101 Captivating Facts
About
TAYLOR SWIFT

101 Captivating Facts
About
TAYLOR SWIFT

The Ultimate Unofficial Quiz and Trivia for Young Super Fans
---

by Lily F. Smith

101 Captivating Facts
About
TAYLOR SWIFT

by Lily F. Smith

First published in 2024 by Paper Haven Store.

Copyright © 2024 Paper Haven Store.

The right of Lily F. Smith to be identified as the author of this work has been asserted by her in accordance with the Copyright, Designs, and Patents Act of 1988.

Cover drawing and watercolor images by Anna Balment
Coloring images by MyMysticMoonShop

All rights reserved. No part of this publication may be reproduced, distributed, or transmitted in any form or by any means, including photocopying, recording, or other electronic methods, without the prior written permission of the publisher or the author.

The content may not be stored in a retrieval system, transmitted, or copied for public or private use, other than for "fair use" as brief quotations embodied in articles and reviews, without the prior permission of the publisher.

No patent liability is assumed with respect to the use of the information contained herein. Although every precaution has been taken in the preparation of this book, the publisher and author assume no responsibility for errors or omissions. Neither is any liability assumed for damages resulting from the use of the information contained herein.

Disclaimer Notice: Please note the information contained within this document is for educational and entertainment purposes only. All efforts have been made to present accurate, up-to-date, reliable, and complete information. No warranties of any kind are declared or implied.

This book belongs to

_____

_____

Contents:

Chapter 1
The Early Years 12

Chapter 2
Rising to Stardom 46

Chapter 3
Q&A's and Fun Facts 82

Chapter 4
Creative Coloring 126

Introduction

Imagine jumping into Taylor Swift's world, uncovering 101 cool facts about her incredible journey. This book is perfect for young fans who want to learn all about their favorite star. From Pennsylvania to global stardom, Taylor's story is one of dreams coming true through hard work and talent. Before the world tours and hit songs, Taylor was just a girl with a dream. Discover how she fell in love with music. Did you know she wrote her first song at a really young age? Or that she convinced her parents to move to Nashville, the heart of country music? Get ready to see how her journey began!

Follow Taylor's rise to fame, from her debut album to her latest hits. Learn about the key moments and challenges she faced to become a superstar. Each album and tour have shaped her career, making her the sensation she is today.

Time for some interactive fun! Test your Taylor knowledge with quizzes about her music, personal stories, and career highlights. Discover fun facts and little-known stories that even big fans might not know. Each question and answer will surprise you!

This book is more than just facts: We dive into Taylor's personality, her highs, lows, and everything in between to show what makes her an icon. Taylor Swift isn't just a singer; she stands for determination and staying true to yourself. Her journey shows the importance of being strong and authentic. Learn what goes on behind the curtain! From songwriting, teaming up with other artists, to unforgettable performances, discover what makes each album and tour so special.

Whether you read the book from start to finish or jump around to your favorite sections, you'll stay hooked. By the end, you'll know more about Taylor's life and feel a deeper connection to her music and story. Enjoy the stories and quizzes, feel inspired to chase your dreams, and remember, Taylor's journey isn't over—each album and tour brings something new. Unleash your artistic side with Taylor Swift-inspired coloring pages! Each page is a celebration of color and creativity, just like Taylor herself! Keep being an awesome fan, keep enjoying her music, and who knows? Maybe your journey will be just as amazing someday! So let's get started, learn about Taylor's legacy, and enjoy this exciting adventure together.

Ready? Let's go!

"It's never been about trying to look
well-behaved. It's just how I am.
I guess it's a weird thing to be 19 and not
ever have been drunk, but for me, it just feels
normal because I don't really know any other
way. I don't know if I'd be comfortable getting
wasted and not knowing what I've said.
That doesn't mean when I'm older
I won't have a glass of wine. I just don't think
it's such a strange thing for me not
to be wasted all the time."

– Taylor Swift

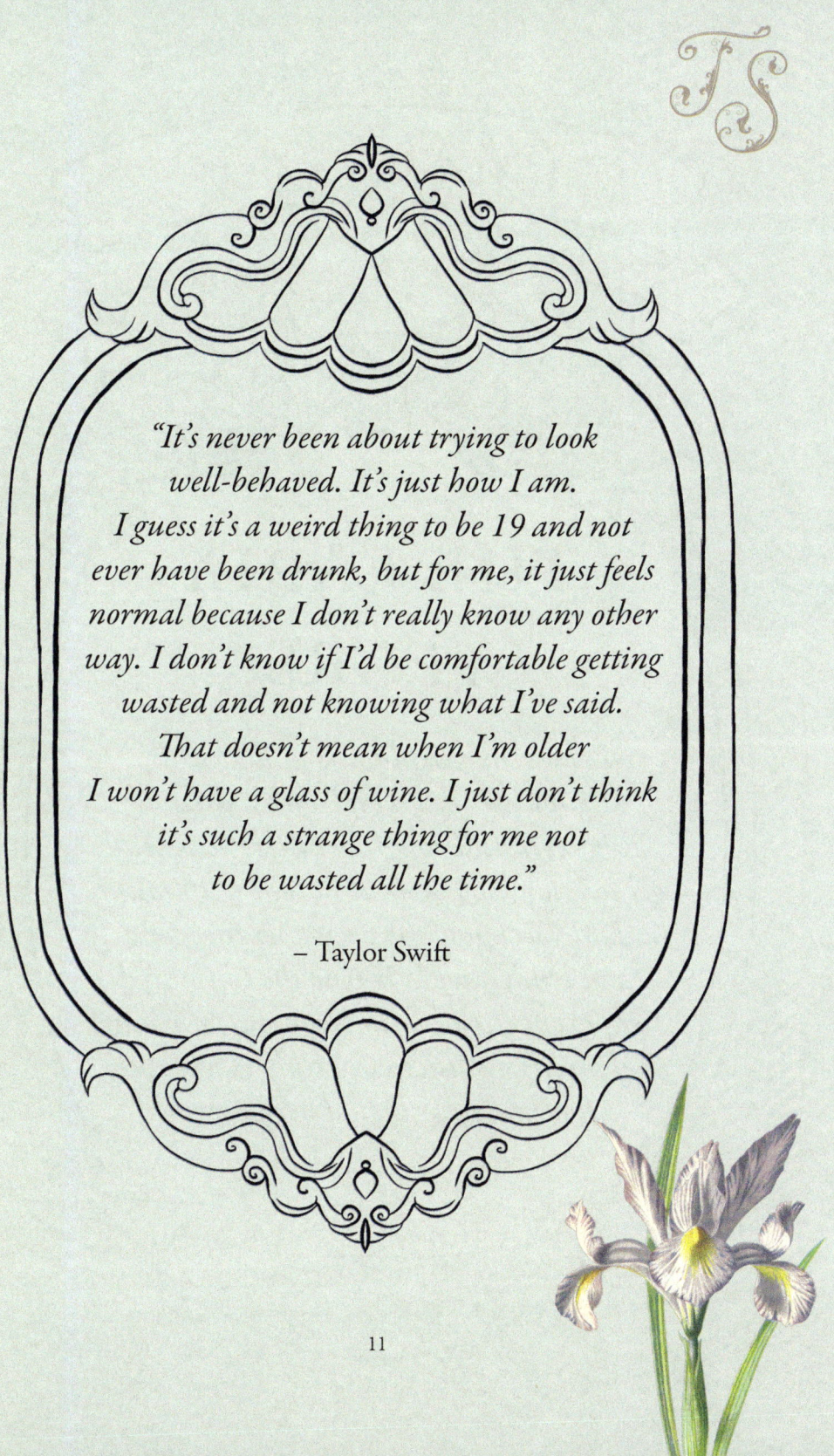

Chapter 1

THE EARLY YEARS

Before the world tours and awards, Taylor was just a girl with a dream. Take a stroll through her early years and get to know how she fell in love with music. Did you know she wrote her first song at a tender age? Or how she convinced her parents to move to Nashville, the heart of country music? Get ready to uncover the amazing start of her journey!

Lily F. Smith

Embarking on a journey through Taylor Swift's early years unveils a captivating tale of family ties and the transformative experiences that sculpted her into the iconic artist she is today. Hailing from the quaint town of Reading, Pennsylvania, Taylor was immersed in a warm and tight-knit family circle that nurtured her musical talents from the get-go. Her rockstar parents, Scott and Andrea Swift, were the ultimate cheerleaders, fostering her love for music with unwavering support and endless encouragement. These familial bonds served as the launchpad for Taylor's meteoric rise, shaping her artistic voyage and embedding values that echo in her every melody.

In this chapter, readers are invited to plunge into the myriad influences that steered Taylor's formative journey. From the unshakable backing of her family and the musical heritage of her grandmother, Marjorie Finlay, to the inspiration drawn from the bucolic landscapes of rural Pennsylvania, each ingredient played a vital part in sculpting her distinct sound and lyrical prowess. The narrative also unfolds the sacrifices and audacious choices made by her parents, including the bold leap to Nashville, propelling her into the heartbeat of the country music realm. These foundational moments signify the genesis of Taylor Swift's genuineness and relatability, traits that have endeared her to a global fanbase.

"I had the most magical childhood, running free and going anywhere I wanted to in my head."

Birth and Family Background Facts

Taylor Swift's early years were a whirlwind of family vibes and quirky adventures that set the stage for her journey as a rising starlet. Hailing from the vibrant town of Reading, Pennsylvania, Taylor was part of a tight-knit clan that cheered on her artistic escapades from day one. Her folks, Scott and Andrea Swift, were the ultimate boost team, fueling her music dreams with a mix of resources and hype. This family bond and the life lessons from her parents set the groundwork for her future triumphs.

The Swift house buzzed with a melange of influences that shaped Taylor's path. Her grandma, Marjorie Finlay, a diva in the opera world, left an indelible mark on Taylor's musical soul. Binge-watching Marjorie's performances, Taylor caught the inspiration bug to strut her stuff. And let's not forget her bro Austin, the film buff, who added a dash of drama to their creative cauldron, turning the Swift haven into a hub of artistic flair.

But it wasn't just family flair that lit up Taylor's world; the rural charm of Pennsylvania painted the backdrop to her early adventures. Days spent on the family tree farm fed her muse with tales of everyday magic that later adorned her lyrics. These influences not only shaped her vibe but also etched in her the art of keeping it real and relatable, qualities that struck a chord with her future fan club. Parental pep talks were the secret sauce to Taylor Swift's rise to music royalty. Recognizing her talent early on, her folks rolled out the red carpet of opportunities. Vocal lessons, acting gigs – you name it, they made it happen. The Swift mobile became the ride to local gigs and showdowns, doubling as the vessel of cheers and moral boosts. Their rock-solid belief in her lit the fires of confidence, propelling Taylor towards the limelight.

A pivotal moment in Taylor's tale was her Nashville dream. At a mere 14 years old, packing up and moving to the country music capital was

TALKING ABOUT HER GRANDMOTHER MARJORIE FINLAY:

"I can remember her singing, the thrill of it. She was one of my first inspirations. The people around me provided all the inspiration I needed. Everything I wrote (at that time) came from that experience, what I observed happening around me."

no small feat. But with grit and gusto, her folks uprooted the clan to Tennessee, marking a new chapter in Taylor's musical saga. This move opened doors to industry bigwigs and iconic stages, like the legendary Bluebird Cafe. Beyond logistical support, Taylor's parents were her pillars of strength during the stormy seas of the music biz. Rejections, setbacks – you name it, they weathered it with her. Offering solace and motivation in tough times, they reminded Taylor of her mettle, urging her to keep chasing her star. This unwavering support system powered Taylor through the highs and lows of the industry with poise and persistence.

Taylor Swift's cultural collage was the kaleidoscope that colored her music and persona. Nestled in a family with rich American heritage, she absorbed an agglomeration of traditions and tales that tinted her worldview. Her rural upbringing sowed the seeds of love for country music, the cornerstone of her early tunes. Themes of small-town charm, personal anecdotes, and heartfelt yarns pepper her music, reflecting her roots and soulful storytelling. This rich cultural background deeply influences Taylor's songwriting brilliance. Her knack for spinning tales into tunes stems from the storytelling ethos she grew up with. Whether serenading teenage romances or narrating heartaches, her lyrics carry a rawness and realness that speaks to souls far and wide. This blend of personal chronicles and cultural hues cements her place as a storyteller extraordinaire in the world of melodies.

Moreover, Taylor's cultural compass shapes her public aura and ethos. Grounded and connected to her fans, she credits her roots for keeping her feet firmly on the ground amid the stardom spiral. This authenticity echoes in her music, spilling over into her philanthropic missions and advocacy for causes dear to her heart. By staying true to her heritage while embracing the diverse cultural mosaic, Taylor Swift has carved a niche in the music world, fusing tradition with modern flair to captivate a rainbow of hearts.

Early Musical Influences and Beginnings in Songwriting

Taylor Swift's early musical influences were a blend of various genres and artists, which significantly molded her unique style. Growing up in Pennsylvania, she was exposed to country music through artists like Shania Twain and the Dixie Chicks, who were some of her mother's favorites. These artists not only influenced her vocal style but also instilled a love for storytelling through song lyrics. Taylor often mentioned how their music made her feel emotions that she wanted to replicate in her own work.

Beyond country, Taylor showed an interest in other genres as well. She listened to pop icons like Britney Spears and Christina Aguilera, whose energetic performances and catchy melodies intrigued her. This mix of country narrative depth and pop accessibility became a cornerstone of her musical identity. Her ability to blend these styles would later distinguish her from other artists and help her stand out in a competitive industry.

Moreover, Taylor's appreciation for classic rock bands like The Beatles and Fleetwood Mac added another layer to her musical understanding. She admired their intricate melodies and harmonies, which inspired her to experiment with different sounds and structures in her songwriting. This eclectic taste in music allowed her to draw from a rich palette of influences, setting the stage for her versatile and adaptive career.

Moving on to Taylor Swift's songwriting process, it became clear that storytelling was at the heart of her songs. From a young age, she was keenly observant, writing down her thoughts and experiences in journals. These entries often served as raw material for her lyrics, capturing the authenticity and vulnerability that fans found relatable.

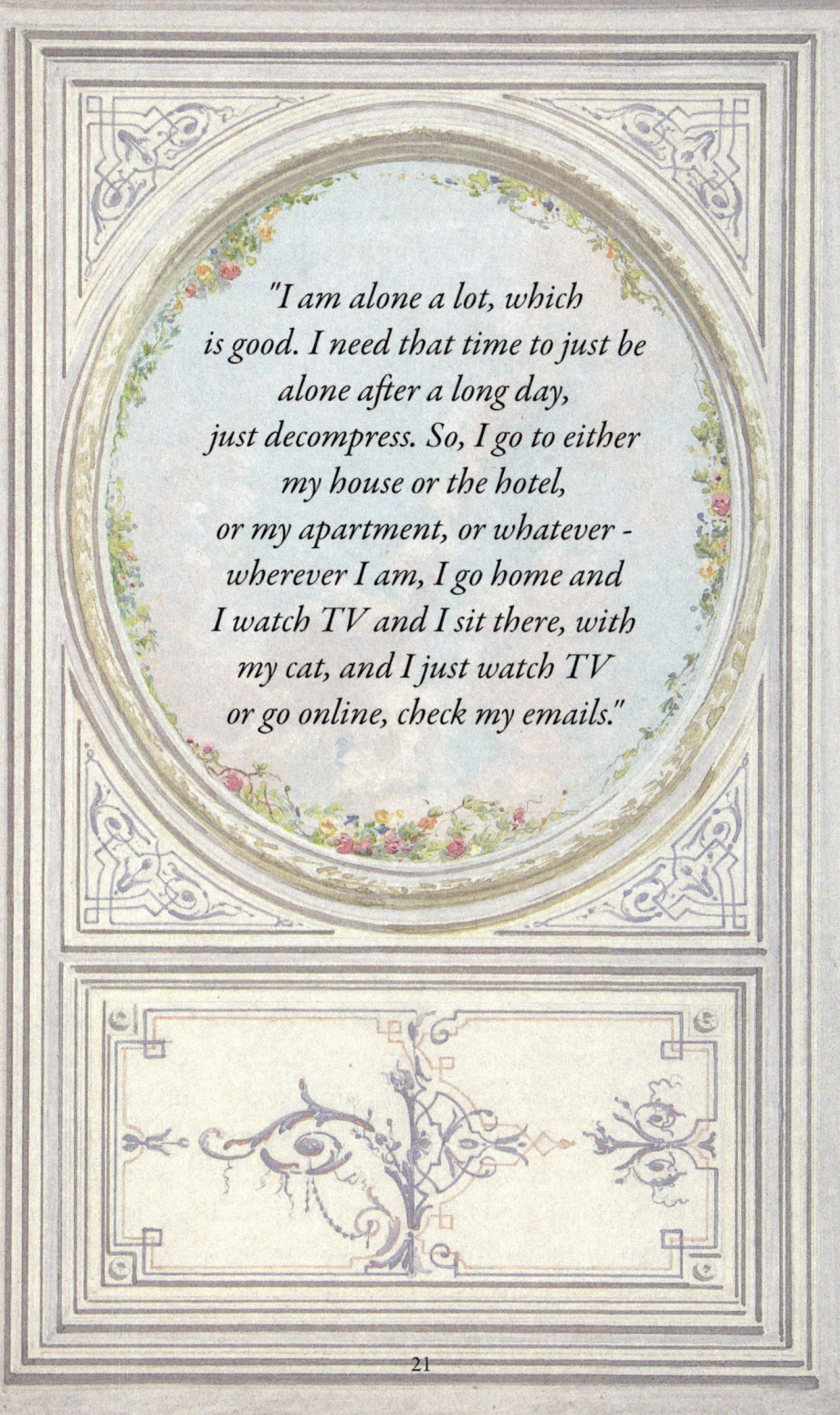

"I am alone a lot, which
is good. I need that time to just be
alone after a long day,
just decompress. So, I go to either
my house or the hotel,
or my apartment, or whatever -
wherever I am, I go home and
I watch TV and I sit there, with
my cat, and I just watch TV
or go online, check my emails."

Taylor's approach was intensely personal; she used songwriting as a means to process her feelings and connect with listeners on an emotional level.

In her formative years, Taylor would often sit down with her guitar and let her emotions guide her fingers across the strings. She has described her songwriting as a cathartic experience, where melodies and lyrics would flow naturally when she immersed herself in her feelings. This spontaneous yet heartfelt method resulted in songs that resonated deeply with both her peers and older audiences alike.

Taylor's commitment to honesty in her lyrics is another hallmark of her songwriting process. She didn't shy away from sharing intimate details about her life, whether it was about teenage heartbreaks or learning experiences. This candidness helped her build a loyal fan base who saw her songs as a soundtrack to their own lives. It also showcased her maturity as a songwriter, enabling her to tackle more complex themes as she grew older.

The creative evolution of Taylor Swift's songwriting is a fascinating journey that showcases her growth as an artist. In her early days, her songs were simple yet evocative, often centered around universal themes like love and friendship. Tracks like *"Tim McGraw"* and *"Teardrops on My Guitar"* exemplify this period, combining straightforward melodies with poignant lyrics that appealed to a wide audience. These early works laid the groundwork for her signature style: emotionally charged storytelling set to memorable tunes.

As she progressed in her career, Taylor's songwriting began to reflect her evolving perspectives and experiences. Albums like *"Fearless"* and *"Speak Now"* demonstrated greater lyrical depth and complexity, tackling issues such as self-discovery and empowerment. Collaborations with co-writers like Liz Rose further enriched her music, bringing new dimensions to her sound and narrative techniques. This phase marked a significant step in her artistic journey, showing her willingness to explore and reinvent herself.

Lily F. Smith

"Well, I do sleep well at night knowing that I'm right and knowing that in 10 years it will have been a good thing that I spoke about artists' rights to their art, and that we bring up conversations like: Should record deals maybe be for a shorter term, or how are we really helping artists if we're not giving them the first right of refusal to purchase their work if they want to?"

"I think songwriting is the ultimate form of being able to make anything that happens in your life productive."

"When I was a little girl I used to read fairy tales. In fairy tales you meet Prince Charming and he's everything you ever wanted. In fairy tales the bad guy is very easy to spot. The bad guy is always wearing a black cape so you always know who he is. Then you grow up and you realize that Prince Charming is not as easy to find as you thought. You realize the bad guy is not wearing a black cape and he's not easy to spot; he's really funny, and he makes you laugh, and he has perfect hair.

"When I was growing up, I didn't really know much about being popular or cliques or anything like that. In elementary school and middle school, you start to kind of realize what it's all about. There are cool kids, and then there's you, and you're just trying to figure out where you fit in. I learned a lot about acceptance and rejection, Those are the themes that you'll find spread throughout my music and weaved in throughout all of the lyrics. I really know what it's like to be accepted, and I also know what it's like to be rejected. And those are lessons I learned in Wyomissing."

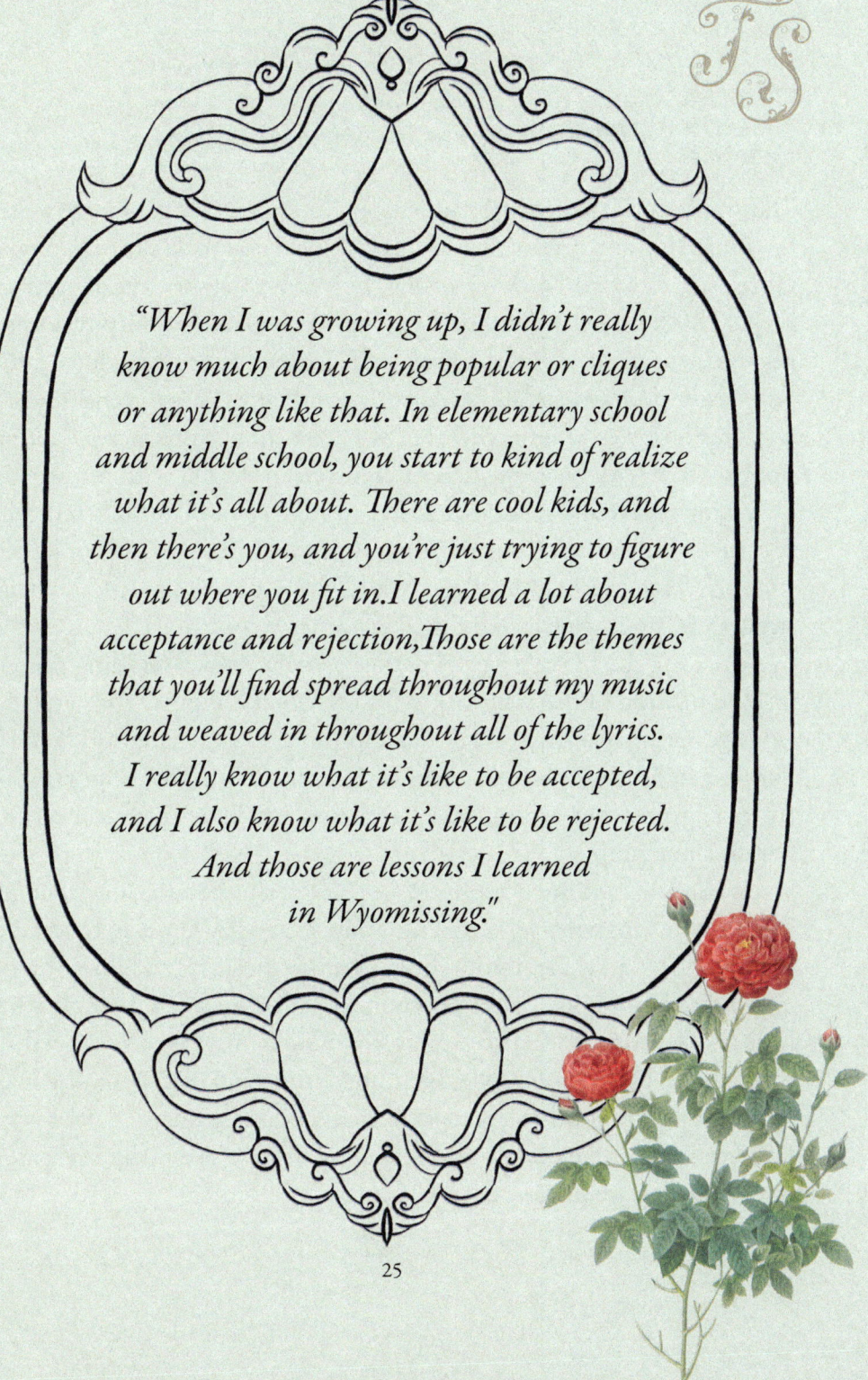

Initial Steps Towards a Music Career Including Early Performances

The journey of Taylor Swift's musical pursuits began at a young age when her innate passion for music started to shine through. Growing up on a Christmas tree farm in Wyomissing, Pennsylvania, she experienced an idyllic childhood that provided her with the space and inspiration to nurture her talents. At just ten years old, Taylor performed at local fairs, festivals, and karaoke contests, capturing audiences with her enthusiasm and vocal prowess. Her early love for performing wasn't just a fleeting hobby—it was a sign of the deeper connection she felt with music.

Taylor's parents recognized her potential and supported her dreams wholeheartedly, providing both emotional and practical support. Her mother, Andrea, would drive her to countless talent shows and singing lessons, while her father, Scott, played a vital role in managing the business aspects that came with her budding career. The dedication and hard work paid off when Taylor was invited to sing the national anthem at a Philadelphia 76ers game, marking one of her first significant performances on a larger stage. This opportunity further ignited her aspirations, validating her belief that music was her destined path.

As Taylor continued to hone her skills, she became increasingly involved in songwriting, spending hours every day crafting lyrics and melodies. She drew inspiration from country music legends like Shania Twain and Faith Hill, whose storytelling abilities resonated deeply with her. This period of intensive practice and exploration was crucial in forming Taylor's unique style, blending traditional country influences with her fresh, youthful perspective. It became evident that Taylor Swift wasn't just passionate about singing—she was equally dedicated to becoming a well-rounded musician and performer.

When it comes to performance milestones, Taylor Swift's journey is marked by a series of impactful steps. Initially, she played at small venues around her hometown, such as coffee shops, bookstores, and community gatherings. These intimate settings allowed her to connect with audiences on a personal level, refining her stage presence and gaining confidence with each performance. Her commitment to her craft was unwavering; even as a teenager, she treated every show, regardless of its size, with professionalism and care.

A key turning point came when Taylor was just eleven years old and visited Nashville, Tennessee, the heart of country music. Armed with demo tapes of her karaoke performances, she ambitiously approached record labels along Music Row, seeking any opportunity to get her foot in the door. Though this initial trip didn't result in a record deal, it did lead to valuable contacts and insights into the industry. More importantly, it instilled in Taylor a profound determination to succeed, no matter the obstacles she faced.

Taylor's persistence soon paid off when she began performing at the esteemed Bluebird Café in Nashville, a venue known for discovering new talent. Here, she captured the attention of music industry professionals with her heartfelt performances and original songs. These appearances were instrumental in securing her first publishing deal with Sony/ATV Tree Publishing, making her the youngest signing in the company's history. This achievement not only validated her hard work but also paved the way for her eventual breakthrough in the music industry.

Audience reception plays a pivotal role in understanding Taylor Swift's early career trajectory. Her very first public performances were met with a mix of curiosity and admiration as locals observed a young girl with immense talent and stage presence far beyond her years. The genuine emotion in her voice and lyrics resonated strongly with listeners, many of whom could relate to the themes of love, heartbreak, and growing up woven throughout her songs. It was clear that Taylor had a special ability to connect with people through her music.

"If you're horrible to me, I'm going to write a song about it, and you won't like it. That's how I operate."

As Taylor's visibility increased, so did the positive response from audiences. Her open mic nights and talent show wins started to build a buzz around her name within her community and beyond. One significant moment came with the release of her debut single, "*Tim McGraw*", which quickly gained traction on country radio stations. The song's poignant lyrics and memorable melody struck a chord with listeners, marking the start of her ascent in the country music scene. Fans appreciated her authenticity and the way she seamlessly blended personal experiences with universal emotions.

The early acclaim Taylor received laid the foundation for her future success. Critics praised her songwriting ability, noting that despite her youth, she possessed a maturity and depth that set her apart from other emerging artists. This positive feedback bolstered her confidence and solidified her reputation as a promising young talent. As her fan base grew, so did the anticipation for her forthcoming projects, setting the stage for what would become a spectacular career in music.

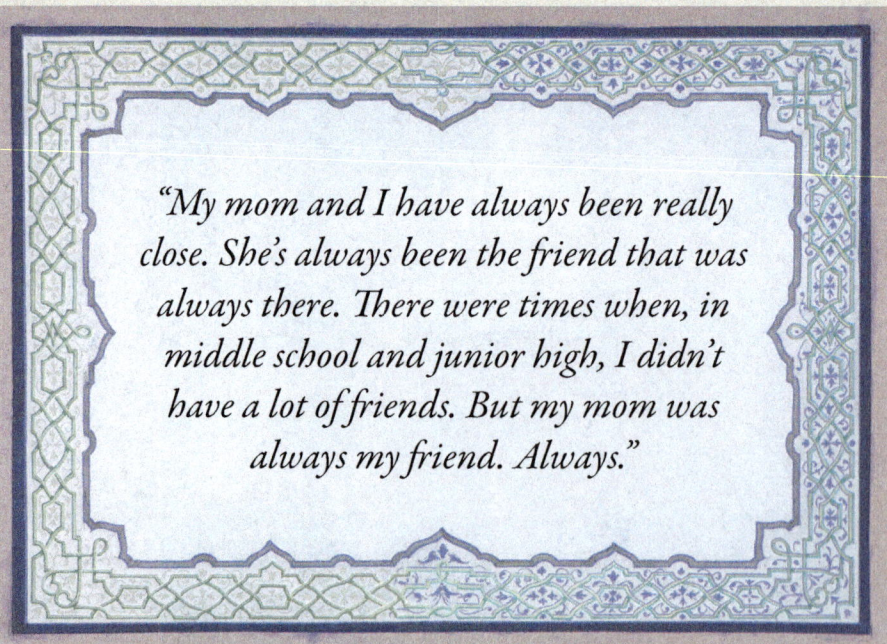

"My mom and I have always been really close. She's always been the friend that was always there. There were times when, in middle school and junior high, I didn't have a lot of friends. But my mom was always my friend. Always."

Relocation to Nashville and Signing with Her First Record Label

Taylor Swift's decision to move to Nashville was a pivotal moment in her life and career. Nashville is often called the "Music City" for a reason, serving as a hub for country music and housing some of the most famous recording studios and record labels in the industry. Taylor recognized that to succeed in country music, she needed to be where the action was. Her choice to relocate to Nashville was driven by the city's vibrant music scene and its reputation for nurturing and launching new artists. This move represented a significant commitment to her musical aspirations.

Nashville provided Taylor with numerous opportunities to immerse herself in the music industry. She attended songwriting sessions, performed at local venues, and networked with industry professionals. The city's culture of collaboration and creativity allowed her to hone her songwriting skills and connect with other musicians. Here, Taylor found a community that shared her passion for music and supported her dreams. These experiences were instrumental in shaping her early career and solidifying her place in the country music scene.

The environment in Nashville also played a crucial role in Taylor's growth as an artist. Surrounded by talented songwriters and performers, she was inspired to push her creative boundaries. The city's rich musical history and ongoing innovation motivated her to refine her talent and strive for excellence. By making Nashville her base, Taylor positioned herself at the heart of the music industry, gaining access to resources and experiences that would propel her career forward.

The announcement of Taylor Swift's first record deal was a major milestone in her journey. Before securing this deal, Taylor faced challenges common to many aspiring artists. She performed at countless

101 Captivating Facts About Taylor Swift

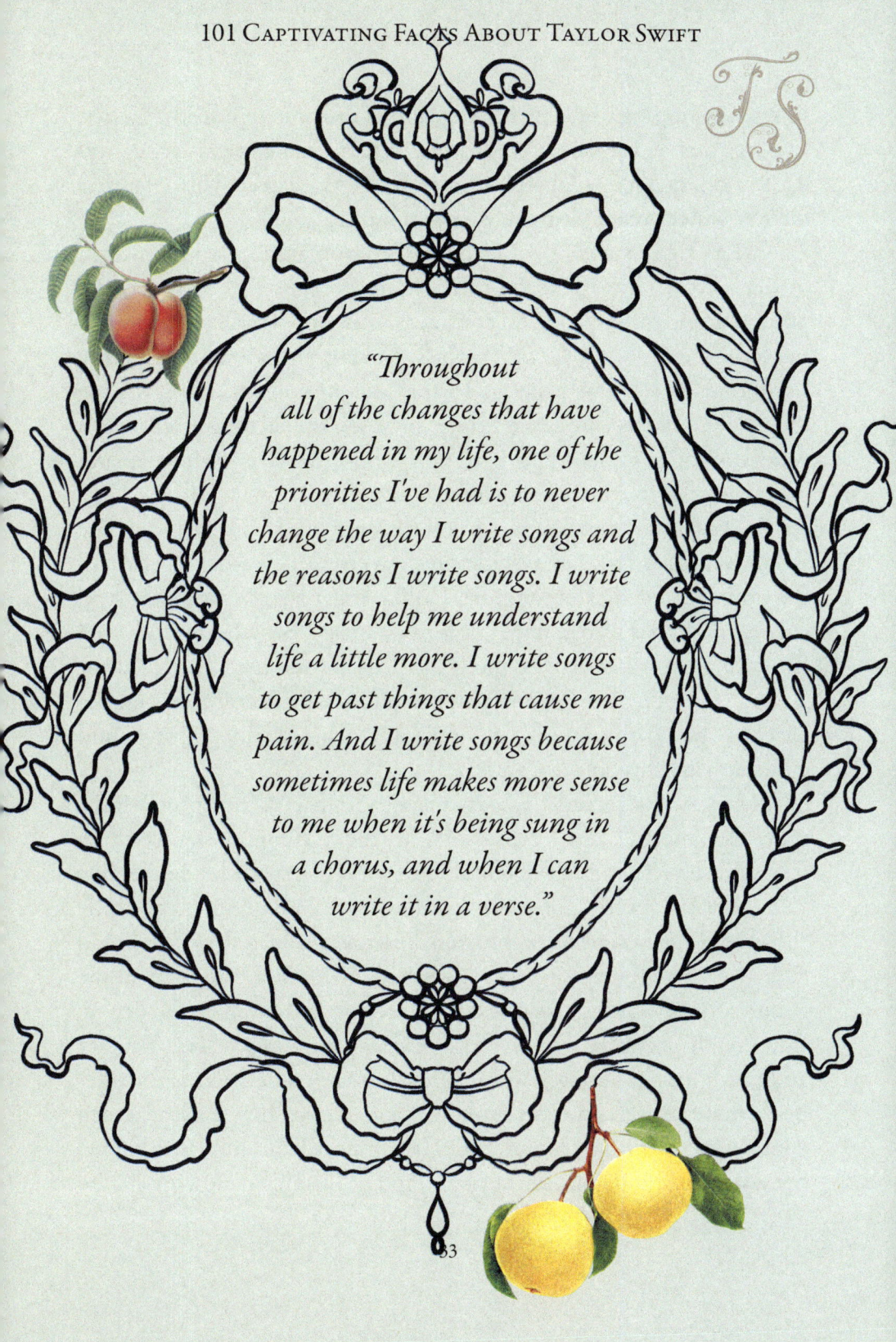

"Throughout all of the changes that have happened in my life, one of the priorities I've had is to never change the way I write songs and the reasons I write songs. I write songs to help me understand life a little more. I write songs to get past things that cause me pain. And I write songs because sometimes life makes more sense to me when it's being sung in a chorus, and when I can write it in a verse."

showcases, hoping to catch the attention of influential industry figures. During this time, she demonstrated remarkable persistence and dedication, qualities that would later define her career. This relentless pursuit of her dream ultimately led to a breakthrough.

Taylor's signing with Big Machine Records marked the culmination of her efforts. The label's founder, Scott Borchetta, recognized her potential and offered her a contract. This opportunity came after numerous rejections from other labels, making the moment even more significant. Borchetta's belief in Taylor's unique voice and songwriting ability set the stage for her future success. The signing itself was a validation of her talent and hard work, boosting her confidence and energizing her to continue pursuing her goals.

The factors influencing Taylor's decision to sign with Big Machine Records included the label's willingness to give her creative control and the promise of dedicated support. Unlike larger labels that might have tried to mold her into a more marketable image, Big Machine allowed her to maintain her artistic integrity. This autonomy was crucial for Taylor, who valued authenticity in her music. The decision to join Big Machine paved the way for her to develop her distinctive style and connect with fans on a deeper level.

Taylor Swift's record deal significantly impacted her professional trajectory and public perception. With the backing of Big Machine Records, she released her debut album, which featured hit singles like *"Tim McGraw"* and *"Teardrops on My Guitar"*. These songs not only showcased her songwriting prowess but also resonated with a broad audience. The album's success established Taylor as a rising star in the country music world, garnering critical acclaim and commercial success. Entering the industry with a record deal also meant increased visibility and promotional opportunities for Taylor. She gained access to larger performance venues, media coverage, and award shows, all of which contributed to raising her profile. The support from her label helped her navigate the complexities of the music business, allowing her to

focus on her artistry. As her popularity grew, so did the demand for her music, leading to sold-out tours and a growing fanbase.

The pivotal role of Taylor Swift's early life and career decisions in shaping her path to becoming a successful musician

Taylor Swift's journey is truly inspiring, filled with pivotal moments that shaped her career and her as a person. From the close-knit family support she received in Reading, Pennsylvania, to the rich cultural and musical influences that surrounded her, it's clear that Taylor's early years were instrumental in her development as an artist.

Her family's unwavering belief in her talent played a crucial role in her rise to stardom. Scott and Andrea Swift provided not only emotional support but also made significant sacrifices, including relocating the entire family to Nashville so Taylor could chase her dreams. This bold move proved to be a turning point, opening up opportunities for Taylor to network with industry professionals and perform at iconic venues like the Bluebird Café.

Influenced by a diverse range of music—from the storytelling prowess of country legends like Shania Twain to the energetic pop style of Britney Spears—Taylor crafted a unique sound that set her apart. Her ability to blend different genres while maintaining authentic, relatable lyrics quickly resonated with listeners, helping her build a loyal fan base.

Taylor's songwriting journey began in her childhood journal entries, which transformed into songs full of raw emotion and personal experiences. Her commitment to honesty in her lyrics allowed fans to connect deeply with her music, seeing their own stories reflected in her words. This relatability became one of her greatest strengths, securing her place in the hearts of many.

Her path wasn't easy, though. Taylor faced numerous challenges and rejections before landing her record deal with Big Machine Records. Performances at local venues and relentless pursuit of her dreams eventually led to this breakthrough. Scott Borchetta's recognition of her potential and his willingness to give her creative control were key factors in her decision to sign with Big Machine, proving to be a perfect match.

The impact of this record deal was immense. Taylor's debut album featuring hits like *"Tim McGraw"* and *"Teardrops on My Guitar"* skyrocketed her to fame, garnering both critical and commercial success. With increased visibility and promotional opportunities, she quickly became a household name. This success paved the way for sold-out tours and a rapidly growing fan base.

Reflecting on Taylor Swift's foundational moments, it's evident that her talent, perseverance, and the support system around her were crucial in shaping her illustrious career. Her story highlights the importance of family, the power of persistence, and the magic of staying true to oneself.

As we explore more of Taylor's story, it's exciting to see how her early experiences might shape her future work. The genuine and relatable qualities that have always been a part of her music will likely stay key to her creative journey, inviting us to be part of her amazing adventure.

Take-Away Facts
Recap Chapter 1

Fact 1: Taylor Swift was born in West Reading, Pennsylvania.

Fact 2: She grew up in a supportive, close-knit family.

Fact 3: Her parents, Scott and Andrea Swift, played a pivotal role in nurturing her talents.

Fact 4: Her grandmother, Marjorie Finlay, was an opera singer who significantly influenced Taylor.

Fact 5: Taylor was inspired to pursue music after watching videos of her grandmother's performances.

Fact 6: She has a younger brother, Austin, who is interested in film and theater.

Fact 7: Taylor spent her childhood on her family's Christmas tree farm, influencing her storytelling.

Fact 8: Growing up in rural Pennsylvania nurtured her creativity and provided inspiration from everyday moments.

Fact 9: Her family supported her by driving her to local events and competitions.

Fact 10: At age 14, her family relocated to Nashville, Tennessee, to support her musical ambitions.

Fact 11: Taylor's parents enrolled her in vocal and acting classes to help hone her skills.

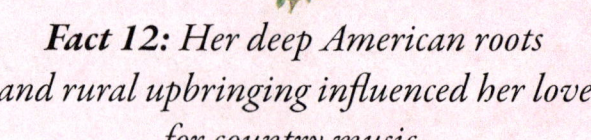

Fact 12: Her deep American roots and rural upbringing influenced her love for country music.

Fact 13: Taylor's music often reflects themes of small-town life and heartfelt storytelling.

Fact 14: She strives to maintain authenticity and relatability in her work.

Fact 15: Her upbringing taught her the importance of staying grounded.

Fact 16: Her family's support was crucial during the challenging parts of her career.

Fact 17: TInfluenced by country music artists like Shania Twain and the Dixie Chicks, who were her mother's favorites.

Fact 18: These artists influenced her vocal style and storytelling abilities.

Fact 19: She was also inspired by pop icons like Britney Spears and Christina Aguilera.

Fact 20: Taylor admired classic rock bands like The Beatles and Fleetwood Mac, inspiring her experimentation with melodies and harmonies.

Fact 21: She used journals to capture thoughts and experiences for her lyrics.

Fact 22: Taylor described her songwriting as a cathartic experience.

Fact 23: TShe committed to honesty in her lyrics, sharing intimate details about her life.

Fact 24: This authenticity helped her build a loyal fan base.

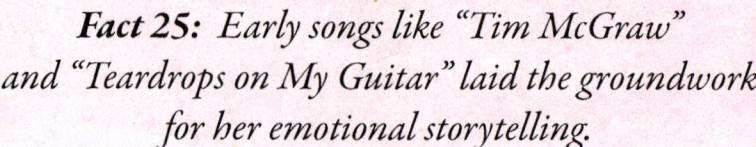

Fact 25: Early songs like "Tim McGraw" and "Teardrops on My Guitar" laid the groundwork for her emotional storytelling.

Fact 26: Collaborating with co-writers like Liz Rose enriched her music.

Fact 27: Taylor performed at small venues like coffee shops and community gatherings to gain confidence and refine her stage presence.

Fact 28: At 11, a visit to Nashville with demo tapes led her to crucial industry contacts.

Fact 29: Performing at the Bluebird Café in Nashville captured the attention of music industry professionals.

Fact 30: Her performances at Bluebird Café paved the way for her career breakthrough.

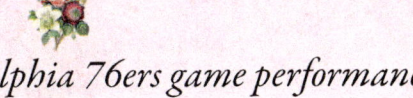

Fact 31: Her Philadelphia 76ers game performance was a significant milestone.

Fact 32: Positive feedback from early performances bolstered her confidence.

Fact 33: The decision to move to Nashville was driven by the city's reputation as a hub for country music.

Fact 34: Nashville provided numerous opportunities for her to immerse herself in the music industry.

Fact 35: She attended songwriting sessions and performed at local venues in Nashville.

Fact 36: Nashville's collaborative environment inspired her to refine her talent.

Fact 37: Signing with Big Machine Records was a major turning point in her career.

Fact 38: She faced numerous rejections before landing her record deal.

Fact 39: Scott Borchetta, founder of Big Machine, recognized her potential and offered her a contract.

Fact 40: Taylor appreciated the creative control offered by Big Machine Records.

Fact 41: The record deal allowed her to maintain her artistic integrity.

Fact 42: Her debut album featured hit singles like "Tim McGraw" and "Teardrops on My Guitar."

Fact 43: The Big Machine deal increased her visibility and promotional opportunities.

Fact 44: Financial and emotional support from her family were crucial as they relocated for her career.

Fact 45: Taylor's strong work ethic and keen business acumen were evident early on.

Fact 46: Her audience admired her relatable lyrics and genuine connection with listeners.

Chapter 2

RISING TO STARDOM

Next, we zoom through Taylor's meteoric rise to fame. This chapter catches you up on her career—from her debut album all the way to her latest hits! Learn about the pivotal moments, the turning points, and the challenges she overcame to become a global sensation. Feel the excitement as you read about how each album and tour has shaped her into the superstar she is today.

Taylor Swift's journey to stardom is an inspiring tale of talent, hard work, and staying true to oneself. From the very beginning, when her debut single *"Tim McGraw"* hit the airwaves in 2006, it was clear that Taylor had something special. The song, a heartfelt reflection on a high school romance, resonated deeply with country music fans, introducing them to Taylor's authentic voice and storytelling prowess. Her ability to connect with listeners on a personal level set the stage for her remarkable ascent in the music industry.

Let's explore Taylor Swift's amazing journey from her first album to becoming a global superstar! We'll see how her debut album, *"Taylor Swift"*, won over young fans with its catchy songs and heartfelt words. You'll also discover how hits like *"Love Story"* and *"You Belong with Me"* made her super famous and loved by many beyond just country music fans. Plus, we'll check out how her music style has changed, the big awards she's won, and how she smartly uses social media to connect with all of us and become a pop icon.

Release and Impact of her Self-Titled Debut Album

Taylor Swift's debut single *"Tim McGraw"* marked her entry into the music industry, leaving a significant imprint on country music fans. Released in 2006, the song was a heartfelt reflection of a high school romance, blending relatable lyrics with an evocative melody. Country music enthusiasts were drawn to the authenticity and innocence of her voice, which stood out amidst the prevailing themes of traditional country music. This debut track showcased Swift's ability to connect with listeners through genuine storytelling, setting the stage for her future success.

The reception of *"Tim McGraw"* was overwhelmingly positive, earning Swift a spot on the Billboard Hot Country Songs chart. Fans appreciated the nostalgic elements of the song, which referenced iconic country artist Tim McGraw, creating an emotional bridge between generations of country music lovers. This strategic move not only paid homage to a well-respected figure in the genre but also positioned Swift as a promising new artist capable of honoring the roots of country music while bringing a fresh perspective.

Beyond its chart performance, *"Tim McGraw"* paved the way for Taylor Swift to establish herself among country music fans. The song's success opened doors for her to perform at various venues, introducing her to a wider audience. With each performance, her growing fanbase became more captivated by her unique blend of traditional country sound and contemporary themes, fueling anticipation for her upcoming album.

Taylor Swift's self-titled debut album resonated profoundly with a younger demographic, solidifying her status as a rising star. Many young listeners found themselves reflected in her songs, which touched on themes of teenage love, heartbreak, and personal growth. Swift's ability to capture the essence of adolescent experiences endeared her to this audience, earning her a loyal fanbase that would follow her throughout her career.

The album's relatability extended beyond its lyrical content. The pop-infused country melodies and catchy hooks made her music accessible and appealing to teenagers and young adults. Unlike much of the traditional country music at the time, Swift's songs incorporated a modern twist that drew in fans who might not have otherwise engaged with the genre. This diverse appeal helped her cross generational and genre boundaries, broadening her reach significantly.

Swift's connection with her young fans was further strengthened through her active engagement with them via social media and fan interactions. She often shared personal stories and insights behind her songs, creating a sense of intimacy and relatability. This direct communication bridged the gap between artist and audience, fostering a community where fans felt genuinely understood and valued, contributing to their unwavering loyalty.

One of the defining aspects of Taylor Swift's debut album was the incorporation of personal experiences in her song lyrics. From the heartache of a teenage romance in *"Teardrops on My Guitar"* to the yearning expressed in *"Picture to Burn"*, Swift's songwriting was a window into her life. This vulnerability and honesty in her music resonated deeply with listeners, who saw their own lives mirrored in her stories.

By sharing her personal experiences, Swift created a space where fans could find solace and companionship. Her lyrics offered comfort and validation to those experiencing similar emotions, making her music both a soundtrack and a source of support. The authenticity of her storytelling set her apart from many contemporaries, establishing her as not just a singer but a relatable figure whom fans could trust and admire.

This approach to songwriting also highlighted Swift's skill as a storyteller. Her narratives were rich with detail and emotion, painting vivid pictures that drew listeners into her world. Each song was like a diary entry, filled with raw emotion and candid reflections. This unique blend of personal transparency and artistic craftsmanship cemented her reputation as a talented songwriter, capable of transforming her own experiences into universally relatable art.

Swift's debut album garnered significant award nominations and wins, acknowledging her talent and hard work. The recognition began with nods from prestigious country music institutions such as the Academy of Country Music and the Country Music Association. These nominations served as a testament to her musical prowess and hinted at the bright future that lay ahead.

At the 2007 CMT Music Awards, Swift won the Breakthrough Video of the Year for *"Tim McGraw"*. This accolade was a crucial stepping stone, affirming her impact on the music industry and her potential as a major player within it. The award not only boosted her visibility but also validated her efforts, encouraging her to continue pushing creative boundaries.

Breakthrough Years with 'Fearless' and Subsequent Albums

Taylor Swift's rise to stardom is nothing short of spectacular. Her transition from a promising newcomer to a chart-topping pop sensation can be traced back to the impact of her early hits like *"Love Story"* and *"You Belong with Me"*. These songs were pivotal in catapulting her career and establishing her as a household name. *"Love Story"*, with its catchy melody and fairy-tale narrative, appealed widely to both country and pop audiences. It not only topped country charts but also found significant success on the Billboard Hot 100, reflecting her crossover appeal.

"You Belong with Me" further cemented Taylor's popularity by capturing the angst and hopefulness of young love, resonating deeply with teenagers and young adults. The music video, depicting Taylor as the girl-next-door pining for her crush, struck a chord, earning her extensive airplay on MTV and other music channels. This song's universal theme and relatable storyline showcased her knack for creating music that connects emotionally with listeners, broadening her fan base beyond country music enthusiasts.

The success of these hits set the stage for Taylor's experimentation with different musical genres in subsequent albums. She began blending more pop elements into her country roots, evident in her third studio album, *"Speak Now"*. Songs like *"Mine"* and *"Back to December"* still held onto her country origins while exploring broader pop structures and production styles. This period marked her growth as an artist willing to take risks and push genre boundaries, appealing to an even wider audience.

Her willingness to experiment became more pronounced with the release of *"Red"*. This album was a bold move, featuring collaborations

with pop producers and integrating diverse musical influences. Tracks like *"We Are Never Ever Getting Back Together"* and *"I Knew You Were Trouble"* showcased a polished pop sound, moving away from traditional country instrumentation. *"Red"* was a commercial success, debuting at number one on the Billboard 200 and receiving critical acclaim for its maturity and depth, proving that Taylor could successfully navigate multiple genres while maintaining her identity.

Taylor's exploration didn't stop there. With *"1989"*, she made a definitive shift towards mainstream pop, an evolution that was both strategic and artistic. The album was a complete overhaul of her sound, fully embracing synth-pop and collaborating with top-notch producers like Max Martin. Singles such as *"Shake It Off"* and *"Blank Space"* dominated the charts and marked her arrival as a pop powerhouse. The tour supporting *"1989"* broke records worldwide, highlighting her ability to captivate large audiences with her new sound.

The critical and commercial success of albums like *"Speak Now"* and *"Red"* demonstrated Taylor's adeptness at evolving her music while staying true to her storytelling roots. *"Speak Now"* was entirely self-written, showcasing her songwriting prowess and personal touch. It received positive reviews for its authenticity and lyrical sophistication. The album's success bolstered her reputation as a serious artist capable of producing hit records without compromising her artistic integrity.

Similarly, *"Red"* was a milestone that highlighted her transitional phase from country starlet to a multi-genre artist. Its eclectic mix of sounds – from pop and rock to folk and electronic – illustrated her versatility and willingness to experiment. The emotional depth of songs like *"All Too Well"* and the vibrant energy of tracks like *"22"* catered to a broad spectrum of musical tastes, ensuring its widespread acclaim and robust sales figures.

Taylor's exploration of personal growth and relationships in her music has been a consistent theme throughout her career. Her lyrics often delve into her own experiences, making her songs relatable and heartfelt. In *"Speak Now"*, tracks like *"Dear John"* and *"Last Kiss"* provided intimate glimpses into her personal life, articulating feelings of heartbreak and reflection. This openness endeared her to fans, who found solace and connection in her candid storytelling.

With *"Red"*, Taylor continued this trend, navigating the complexities of adult relationships and personal development. Songs like *"Begin Again"* reflected a sense of renewal and introspection, while *"Holy Ground"* celebrated past relationships with a nostalgic yet positive outlook. These narratives showcased her growth not just as an artist but as an individual, resonating with fans experiencing similar transitions in their lives.

Her later albums, including *"1989"* and beyond, maintained this exploration of personal themes with increasing sophistication. *"Clean"*, a track from *"1989"*, symbolized emotional recovery and strength, illustrating her evolution from a young singer-songwriter to a mature artist who could convey profound themes through her music. This continuous thematic development has kept her music relevant and impactful, allowing her to maintain a strong connection with her audience over the years.

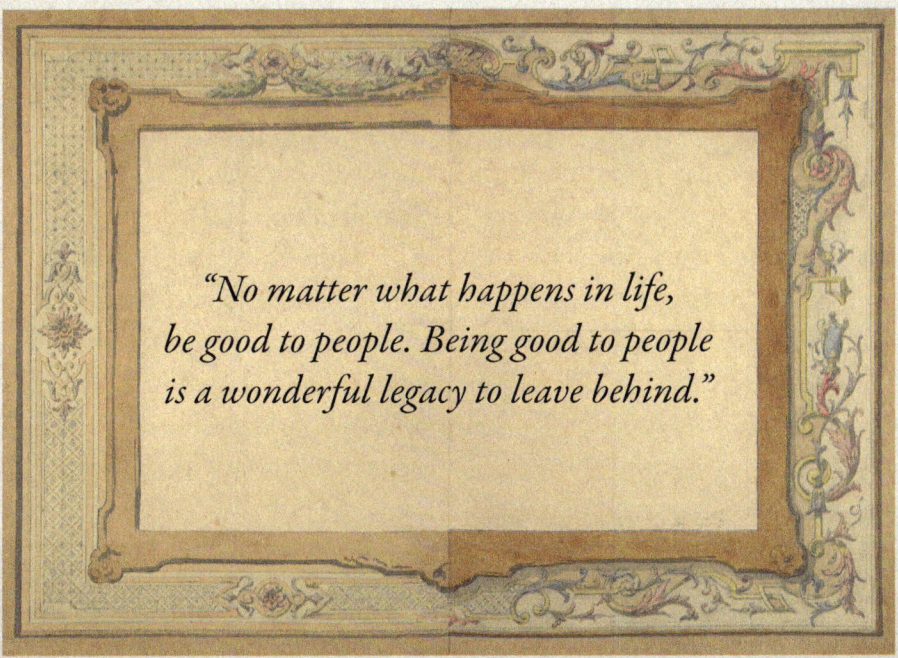

"No matter what happens in life, be good to people. Being good to people is a wonderful legacy to leave behind."

Major Awards and Recognitions During this Period

Winning the Album of the Year Grammy for *'Fearless'* was a pivotal moment in Taylor Swift's career, marking her arrival as a major player in the music industry. This award not only validated her talent and hard work but also had a profound cultural impact. It underlined a shift in musical tastes and opened doors for country-pop crossover artists. The recognition meant that a young artist from a relatively niche genre could achieve mainstream success, influencing many aspiring musicians to explore beyond their traditional boundaries.

The significance of this win cannot be overstated. At just 20 years old, Swift became the youngest artist to receive this prestigious award, setting a new benchmark for young women in the music industry. Her triumph resonated broadly, inspiring countless young fans and musicians worldwide to pursue their dreams regardless of age or genre constraints. The win also cemented Swift's reputation as a talented songwriter and performer capable of captivating both critics and fans alike.

Moreover, Swift's victory highlighted the power of narrative-driven songwriting. With *'Fearless'*, she brought deeply personal stories into mainstream music, creating songs that were relatable and emotionally potent. This approach shifted the landscape of pop and country music, encouraging artists to draw from their own lives and experiences, thereby cultivating a more authentic connection with audiences.

Taylor Swift's inclusion in prestigious lists and rankings further solidified her status as a global sensation. Being featured in Forbes' 30 Under 30, Time's 100 Most Influential People, and Billboard's Woman of the Year recognized not just her musical achievements but also her influence and business acumen. These accolades acknowledged her

as an artist who could shape trends and drive conversations across different sectors of society.

Such recognitions also showcased Swift's versatility and ability to constantly evolve while remaining relevant. They reflected her strategic use of social media and digital platforms to engage with fans, making her one of the first artists to fully leverage these tools for career growth. By consistently appearing on these influential lists, Swift demonstrated that she was more than just a singer; she was a multi-faceted icon impacting culture, technology, and business.

Furthermore, these inclusions provided young fans with a role model who exemplified that hard work, innovation, and staying true to oneself could lead to remarkable accomplishments. For young female artists especially, seeing Swift's success challenged industry norms and encouraged them to aim high in their aspirations, fueling a generation of empowered and ambitious musicians.

Media attention around Swift's award show appearances and performances played a crucial role in her rise to prominence. Each appearance was meticulously crafted, often blending theatricality with genuine emotion, leaving a lasting impression on viewers. Her performance at the 2009 MTV Video Music Awards, despite the infamous interruption, is a prime example of how these moments captured public interest and solidified her image as a resilient and formidable artist.

Swift's knack for creating memorable award show moments helped keep her in the public eye. Performances like her duet with Stevie Nicks at the Grammys or the elaborate staging of hits like *"We Are Never Ever Getting Back Together"* demonstrated her commitment to pushing artistic boundaries. These appearances were not just about winning awards but creating spectacles that drew massive media coverage and fan engagement.

This media spotlight also allowed Swift to control her narrative and showcase different facets of her artistry. She used these platforms to not

101 Captivating Facts About Taylor Swift

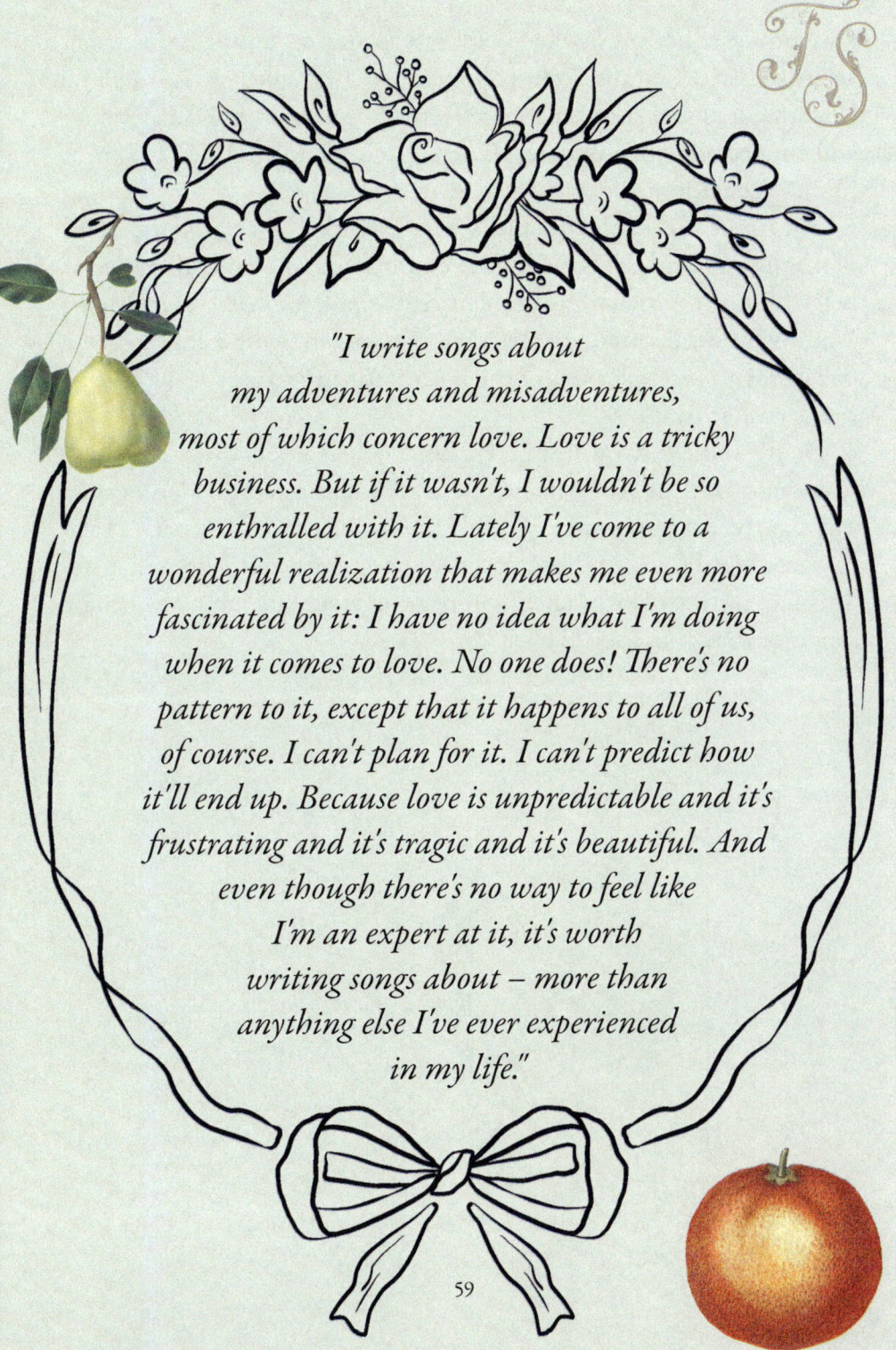

"I write songs about my adventures and misadventures, most of which concern love. Love is a tricky business. But if it wasn't, I wouldn't be so enthralled with it. Lately I've come to a wonderful realization that makes me even more fascinated by it: I have no idea what I'm doing when it comes to love. No one does! There's no pattern to it, except that it happens to all of us, of course. I can't plan for it. I can't predict how it'll end up. Because love is unpredictable and it's frustrating and it's tragic and it's beautiful. And even though there's no way to feel like I'm an expert at it, it's worth writing songs about — more than anything else I've ever experienced in my life."

only promote her music but to address issues important to her, such as artistic freedom and industry practices. Through her award show performances and speeches, she effectively communicated her values and connected with a broader audience, reinforcing her role as a voice for her generation.

The ripple effect of Swift's award wins extended far beyond the realm of trophies and titles. Each accolade contributed to a larger narrative of perseverance, creativity, and authenticity, which resonated deeply with aspiring musicians and fans. Young artists saw in Swift a blueprint for navigating the complexities of the music industry while staying true to their artistic vision.

Swift's success story inspired many to believe in their potential, fostering a wave of creativity across various music genres. Her journey highlighted the importance of resilience in the face of adversity, as she navigated challenges and controversies with grace and determination. This had a trickle-down effect, motivating emerging artists to persist despite setbacks and rejections.

"There was nothing left to do when the butterflies turned to dust that covered my whole room."

—1989 (Taylor's Version)

LILY F. SMITH

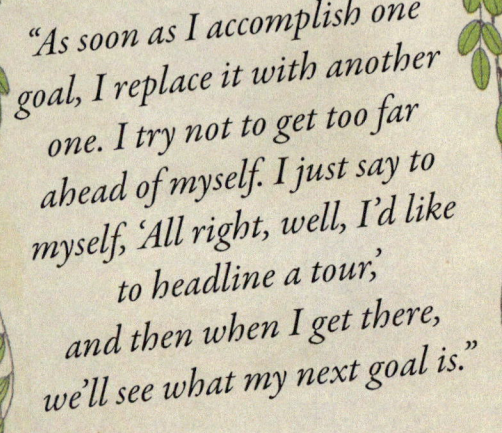

"As soon as I accomplish one goal, I replace it with another one. I try not to get too far ahead of myself. I just say to myself, 'All right, well, I'd like to headline a tour,' and then when I get there, we'll see what my next goal is."

"You can make a board for all the goals you want in your life with the pictures on it, and that's great, daydreaming is wonderful, but you can never plan your future."

"Social media can be great, but it can also inundate your brain with images of what you aren't, how you're failing, or who is in a cooler locale than you at any given moment. One thing I do to lessen this weird insecurity laser beam is to turn off comments. Yes, I keep comments off on my posts. That way, I'm showing my friends and fans updates on my life, but I'm training my brain to not need the validation."

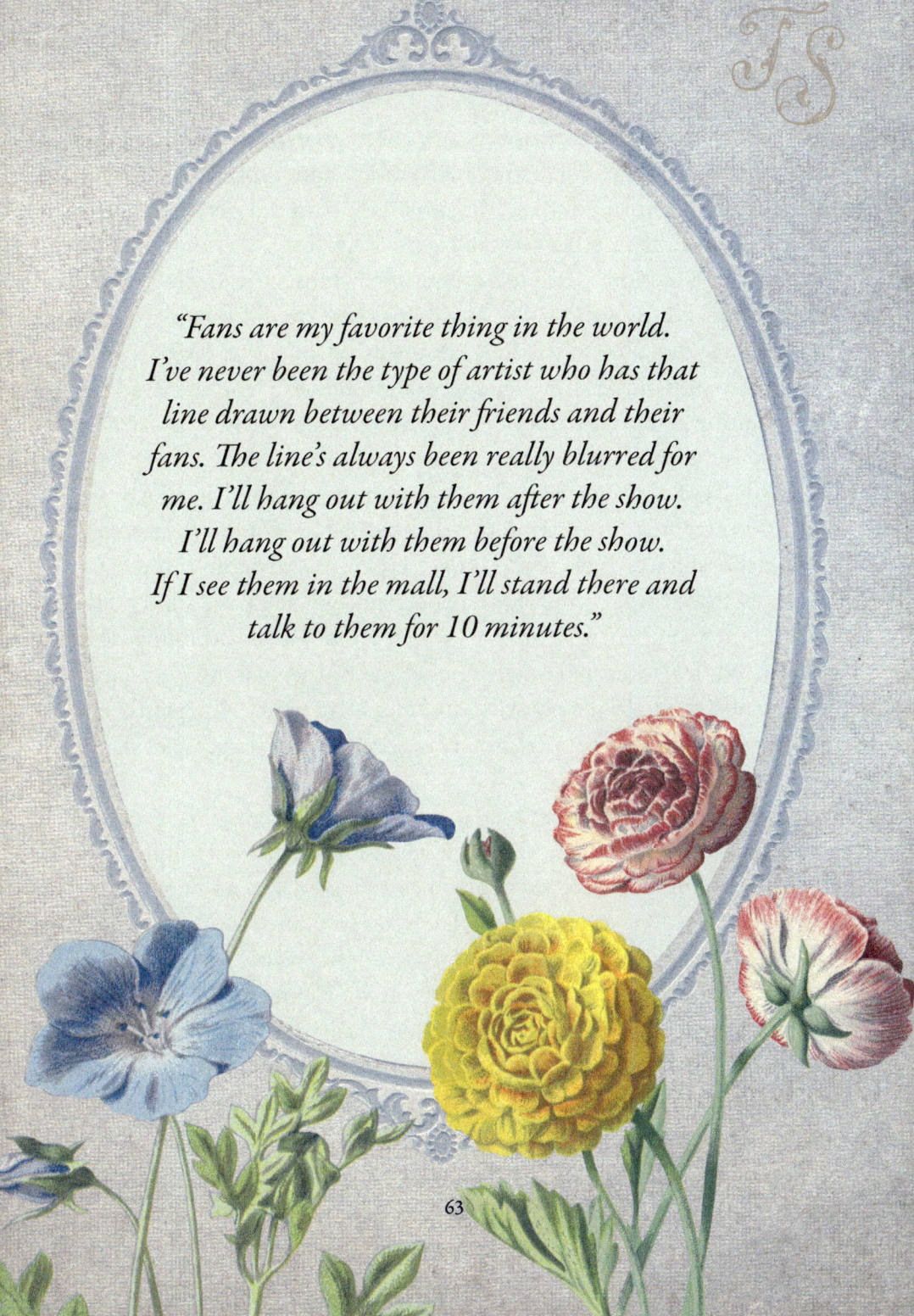

"Fans are my favorite thing in the world. I've never been the type of artist who has that line drawn between their friends and their fans. The line's always been really blurred for me. I'll hang out with them after the show. I'll hang out with them before the show. If I see them in the mall, I'll stand there and talk to them for 10 minutes."

Significant Tours and Milestone Performances

Taylor Swift's live performances are more than just concerts; they are immersive experiences that tell stories and captivate audiences worldwide. From the outset, her tours have featured detailed themes and narratives that reflect her albums. Each tour is a meticulously planned production, designed to transport fans into Taylor's world. For example, during the 1989 World Tour, the overall theme was new beginnings and transformation, encapsulated in her transition from country to pop music. The stages were adorned with vibrant cityscapes, representing different parts of the world, and the setlist was carefully curated to reflect this journey.

In the Reputation Stadium Tour, the narrative focused on rebirth and self-empowerment, mirroring the themes of her album *"Reputation"*. The elaborate sets included massive serpentine structures and dark, gothic aesthetics that symbolized her reclaiming her image amid public scrutiny. These thematic elements weren't just visually stunning; they reinforced the emotional undertones of her music, making the concert experience resonate deeply with attendees. By weaving personal and universal stories into her performances, Taylor created a sense of shared experience among fans.

Furthermore, the Lover Fest tour exemplified themes of love and acceptance, aligned with the messages of her *"Lover"* album. The colorful, whimsical sets and costumes reflected joy and inclusivity, appealing to diverse audiences. Each performance was a carefully crafted narrative journey, allowing fans to connect with Taylor and each other on a meaningful level. These thematic elements are not merely decorative but integral to understanding the artistic vision behind her tours, adding depth and richness to the live concert experience.

Guest appearances by other artists have continually added a layer of excitement and unpredictability to Taylor Swift's concerts. During

the 1989 World Tour, Taylor brought out numerous high-profile guests, from music legends like Mick Jagger to contemporary stars like Selena Gomez. These surprise collaborations not only thrilled fans but also showcased Taylor's ability to bridge different musical genres and generations. Such moments became viral sensations, generating buzz and anticipation for each new show.

Adding these guest appearances wasn't just about star power; it was about enhancing the concert experience. For instance, bringing out her close friend Ed Sheeran during the Red Tour added an intimate, acoustic element to the performances. Fans appreciated the genuine camaraderie and mutual respect between the artists, which translated into memorable, emotionally charged duets. These collaborations enriched the concert narratives, making each performance unique.

Additionally, these guest spots often highlighted Taylor's knack for recognizing and appreciating talent across the music industry. Inviting emerging artists and celebrating their work on such a grand stage demonstrated her influence and support within the music community. These curated moments of collaboration amplified the energy of her shows and underscored her role as a connector of diverse musical talents, further solidifying her position within the entertainment industry.

Taylor Swift's tours have shattered records in attendance and ticket sales, reflecting her immense popularity and the dedicated following she has cultivated over the years. The Reputation Stadium Tour, for example, broke the record for the highest-grossing U.S. tour by a female artist, grossing over $266 million globally. This financial success was also mirrored in incredible audience numbers, with sold-out shows in stadiums worldwide attesting to her powerful draw as a live performer.

The sheer scale of these tours is a testament to her meticulous planning and engagement strategy. Fans often travel great distances and spend significant amounts of money to attend her concerts, a phenomenon noted in various economic impact studies of her tours. Beyond the financial figures, these numbers highlight the cultural significance of

101 Captivating Facts About Taylor Swift

"Getting a great idea with song writing is a lot like love. You don't know why this one is different, but it is. You don't know why this one is better, but it is. It sticks in your head, and you can't stop thinking about it."

her live performances and the dedicated community she has built. Fans' willingness to invest in the concert experience underscores Taylor's ability to create highly anticipated, must-see events.

This overwhelming response is not merely about the numbers but about the quality of the concert experience. The high standards set by Taylor's productions, from flawless vocals to spectacular visuals, ensure that every attendee feels part of something extraordinary. These record-breaking achievements are thus reflective of Taylor's unwavering commitment to delivering top-tier entertainment and her uncanny ability to connect with audiences on a grand scale.

Critical reviews of Taylor Swift's live performances consistently highlight her vocal prowess and stage presence, further cementing her reputation as a consummate performer. Critics frequently praise her ability to deliver powerful vocal performances while maintaining a high-energy stage show. Reviews of her Fearless Tour lauded her for hitting every note with precision and conveying deep emotion through her singing, establishing her early on as a vocalist of note.

Her performances are characterized by their raw emotionality and technical skill, evident in her acoustic sets where her voice is the primary focal point. During the Speak Now World Tour, critics marveled at her ability to switch seamlessly between energetic dance numbers and poignant ballads, showcasing her versatility as a performer. This balance of spectacle and sincerity is a hallmark of Taylor's concerts, providing audiences with a varied and engaging show.

Never be so kind,
you forget to be clever.
Never be so clever,
you forget to be kind.

Never be so polite,
you forget your power.
Never wield such power,
you forget to be polite.

—"Marjorie"

A journey to be appreciated

Taylor Swift's journey from her debut album to becoming a global sensation is nothing short of amazing. Her first single *"Tim McGraw"* introduced her as a fresh voice in country music, connecting deeply with fans through heartfelt storytelling. This early success laid the groundwork for what would become an incredible career.

The impact of *"Tim McGraw"* extended beyond just chart performance; it allowed Taylor to carve out a unique space within the country music scene. She quickly became known for her relatable lyrics and genuine connection with her audience. These elements endeared her to a growing fanbase and hinted at her potential to become a major force in the industry.

As she released her self-titled debut album, Taylor resonated profoundly with young listeners who saw themselves in her songs. The themes of teenage love, heartbreak, and personal growth struck a chord with many, solidifying her status as a rising star. Her ability to blend traditional country sounds with contemporary themes broadened her appeal, bringing in fans from various musical backgrounds.

Throughout this period, Taylor's engagement with her fans played a crucial role. Sharing personal stories and insights behind her songs on social media created a sense of intimacy, making her fans feel genuinely understood and valued. This direct communication strengthened their loyalty and contributed to her rapid rise to fame.

Taylor's knack for incorporating personal experiences into her lyrics set her apart as a storyteller. Songs like *"Teardrops on My Guitar"* and *"Picture to Burn"* offered windows into her life, making her music both relatable and comforting. Fans found solace in her honesty and authenticity, which established her as a trustworthy and admired figure.

Her talent was recognized with award nominations and wins, including her victory at the 2007 CMT Music Awards. Winning

Breakthrough Video of the Year for *"Tim McGraw"* affirmed her impact on the industry and boosted her visibility. These accolades validated her efforts and encouraged her to continue pushing creative boundaries.

From her breakthrough hits like *"Love Story"* and *"You Belong with Me"* to her bold experiments with pop in albums like *"Red"* and *"1989"*, Taylor's evolution showcased her versatility. She successfully navigated different genres while staying true to her roots, proving her ability to captivate a wide audience.

Major awards and recognitions, such as winning the Album of the Year Grammy for 'Fearless,' highlighted her influence and cultural impact. This milestone not only validated her talent but also inspired countless young musicians to pursue their dreams. Her inclusion in prestigious lists like Forbes' 30 Under 30 and Time's 100 Most Influential People further solidified her status as a global icon.

Taylor's live performances have also contributed significantly to her rise. Her meticulous planning and thematic tours create immersive experiences that resonate deeply with fans. Guest appearances and record-breaking ticket sales underscore her immense popularity and the dedicated following she has cultivated.

Through it all, Taylor Swift's unwavering commitment to her craft and her connection with fans have propelled her to unprecedented heights. Her journey from a promising newcomer to a global sensation serves as a source of inspiration for many, showing that with passion and perseverance, one can achieve remarkable success. As Taylor continues to evolve and explore new musical territories, her story remains a testament to the power of authenticity and creativity in the world of music.

Take-Away Facts
Recap Chapter 2

Fact 47: Taylor Swift's debut single "Tim McGraw" was released in 2006 and served as her introduction to the country music scene.

Fact 48: The song reflected a blend of relatable lyrics with an evocative melody.

Fact 49: "Tim McGraw" gained positive reception, earning a spot on the Billboard Hot Country Songs chart.

Fact 50: The song's success positioned Taylor as a promising new artist honoring traditional country music.

Fact 51: Taylor Swift's self-titled debut album resonated deeply with young listeners who connected with themes of teenage love, heartbreak, and personal growth.

Fact 52: Taylor's pop-infused country melodies and catchy hooks made her music appealing to teenagers and young adults.

Fact 53: Her album's relatable content and inclusion of modern twists in country music broadened her fan base.

Fact 54: Taylor actively engaged with her fans via social media, creating a sense of intimacy and community.

Fact 55: Tracks like "Teardrops on My Guitar" and "Picture to Burn" displayed Taylor's ability to incorporate personal experiences into her lyrics.

Fact 56: Her vulnerable and honest storytelling drew fans who found their own lives reflected in her music.

Fact 57: *Taylor's transparent songwriting showcased her as a trustworthy and admired figure.*

Fact 58: *Her success translated into significant award nominations and wins, such as the Breakthrough Video of the Year for "Tim McGraw" at the 2007 CMT Music Awards.*

Fact 59: *Taylor's debut album got her acknowledged by prestigious country music institutions, validating her rising stardom.*

Fact 60: *The songs "Love Story" and "You Belong with Me" from Taylor Swift's "Fearless" album were pivotal in shooting her to stardom.*

Fact 61: *"Love Story" topped country charts and gained significant success on the Billboard Hot 100.*

Fact 62: "You Belong with Me" captured teenage angst, further widening her fan base.

Fact 63: These hits highlighted Taylor's ability to blend country and pop sensibilities.

Fact 64: Taylor began experimenting with different musical genres in albums like "Speak Now" and "Red," integrating more pop elements while retaining her storytelling roots.

Fact 65: "Speak Now," entirely self-written, showed her songwriting prowess and sophistication.

Fact 66: "Red" featured diverse musical influences, marking a transitional phase in her career.

Fact 67: Taylor's collaboration with renowned producers in "Red" and "1989" produced eclectic mixes of sounds, enhancing her commercial appeal.

Fact 68: "1989" signaled a definitive shift to mainstream pop, with singles like "Shake It Off" and "Blank Space" breaking records.

Fact 69: The 1989 World Tour was a massive success, demonstrating her impact as a pop icon.

Fact 70: Taylor's evolution in musical style from "Fearless" to "1989" illustrated her versatility and adaptive nature.

Fact 71: The maturity in her songs like "All Too Well" from "Red" catered to a broad spectrum of tastes and showcased her storytelling skills.

Fact 72: Taylor's lyrics reflect a continuous exploration of personal growth and relationships, resonating widely with her audience.

Fact 73: Songs from "Fearless" to "1989" delve into experiences of heartbreak, self-discovery, and empowerment, providing relatability and emotional resonance.

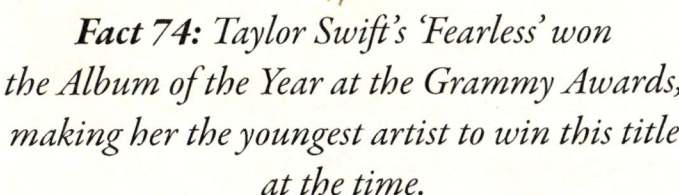

Fact 74: Taylor Swift's 'Fearless' won the Album of the Year at the Grammy Awards, making her the youngest artist to win this title at the time.

Fact 75: Winning the Grammy had a profound cultural impact, validating her talent and opening doors for country-pop crossover artists.

Fact 76: Her Grammy win for 'Fearless' inspired young fans and musicians globally to pursue their dreams.

Fact 77: Taylor was consistently included in prestigious lists like Forbes' 30 Under 30, Time's 100 Most Influential People, and Billboard's Woman of the Year.

Fact 78: These recognitions highlighted her influence, talent, and business acumen.

Fact 79: *Taylor's appearances on influential lists underscored her role as a trendsetter in culture, technology, and business.*

Fact 80: *Award show performances, like those at the MTV Video Music Awards and Grammys, played a key role in Taylor's rise.*

Fact 81: *Memorable moments at award shows, such as high-profile duets, enhanced her visibility and showed her ability to create captivating performance spectacles.*

Fact 82: *Critically acclaimed live performances reiterated her vocal prowess and commanding stage presence.*

Fact 83: *Taylor's thematic and sophisticated conceptualization of her tours set high standards for concert productions.*

Fact 84: *Taylor Swift's tours, such as the 1989 World Tour and Reputation Stadium Tour, were known for their immersive experiences and detailed themes.*

Fact 85: The 1989 World Tour featured vibrant cityscapes narrating themes of new beginnings and transformation.

Fact 86: The Reputation Stadium Tour depicted rebirth and self-empowerment, featuring elaborate sets and gothic aesthetics.

Fact 87: Taylor's Lover Fest illustrated themes of love and acceptance, aligned with her "Lover" album.

Fact 88: Guest appearances by other renowned artists added excitement and depth to her concerts.

Fact 89: Collaborations with artists such as Mick Jagger and Selena Gomez bridged different musical genres and generations, creating viral moments.

Fact 90: Taylor demonstrated support within the music community by inviting emerging artists and recognizing their talents.

Fact 91: *Taylor's tours shattered attendance and ticket sales records, showcasing her immense popularity.*

Fact 92: *The Reputation Stadium Tour became the highest-grossing US tour by a female artist, earning over $266 million globally.*

Fact 93: *Taylor's successful tours and incredible audience numbers happened because of her meticulous planning and engagement strategy.*

Fact 94: *Critics consistently praised her live performances for vocal proficiency and energetic stage presence.*

Fact 95: *Taylor adeptly balanced high-energy dance numbers with poignant ballads during her performances.*

Fact 96: *Taylor's live shows were celebrated for blending personal transparency with artistic ingenuity.*

Fact 97: *Her concerts' aesthetically rich and thematically consistent presentations provided memorable and emotional experiences for fans.*

Fact 98: *Taylor Swift's rise from a promising newcomer to a global sensation is an inspiring journey.*

Fact 99: *Her initial success with singles like "Tim McGraw" established a loyal fan base and spotlighted her distinct voice.*

Fact 100: *Taylor's evolution included strategic genre transitions and continuously exploring personal themes in her music that resonated with diverse audiences.*

Fact 101: *Throughout her career, Taylor maintained authenticity and a strong connection with fans, reinforcing her stature as a global icon.*

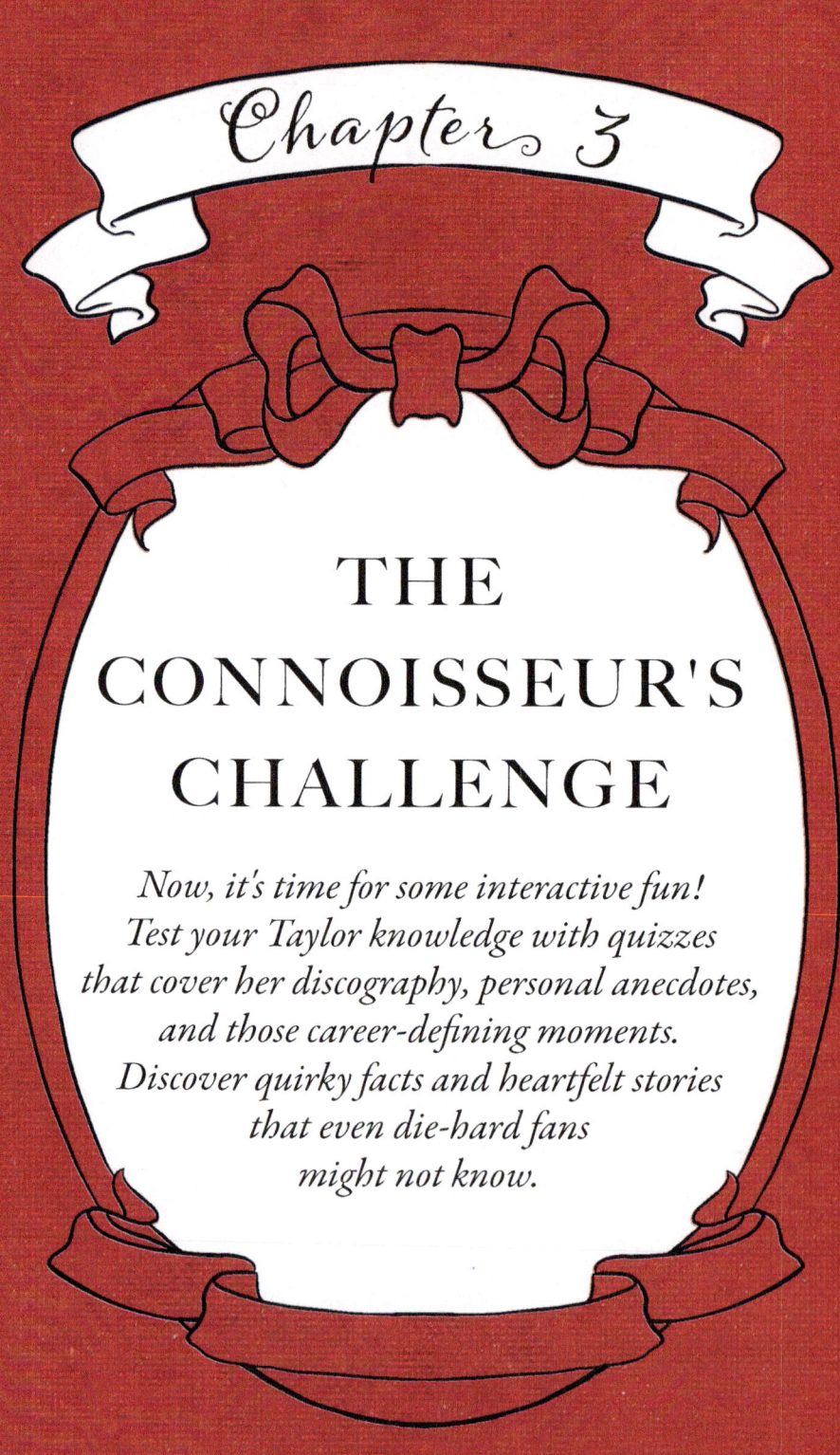

Chapter 3

THE CONNOISSEUR'S CHALLENGE

Now, it's time for some interactive fun! Test your Taylor knowledge with quizzes that cover her discography, personal anecdotes, and those career-defining moments. Discover quirky facts and heartfelt stories that even die-hard fans might not know.

Ready for a fun quiz all about Taylor Swift? If you're a big fan or just curious about her, this will be a blast! Imagine diving into a fun adventure where you peek into the exciting life of Taylor—from her beginnings as a country star to becoming a global pop sensation. In this chapter, you'll get to test how much you know about Taylor while learning cool new facts that even her biggest fans might not know!

Think you can remember the lyrics to her songs or name the artists she's teamed up with? Quiz yourself and see! After each question, you'll get awesome explanations and insights, so you're not just answering questions—you're discovering the fascinating stories behind her music.

You'll explore her albums, learn about the stories behind her famous songs, and even get the scoop on the exciting collaborations she's had. From her high-profile romances to her groundbreaking work in the music industry, there's so much to uncover. As you go through the quiz, you'll not only challenge yourself but also gain a deeper appreciation of how Taylor Swift became the superstar she is today. So get ready for some fun and facts—it's the ultimate Taylor Swift experience!

Section 1: Discography and Albums

1. What was the title of Taylor Swift's debut album?
   - A) "Taylor Swift"
   - B) "Fearless"
   - C) "Red"
   - D) "Speak Now"

2. Which album includes the hit singles "Love Story" and "You Belong with Me"?
   - A) "Speak Now"
   - B) "Red"
   - C) "Fearless"
   - D) "1989"

3. Name the two surprise albums Taylor released during the COVID-19 pandemic.
   - A) "Folklore" and "Lover"
   - B) "Evermore" and "Fearless"
   - C) "Folklore" and "Evermore"
   - D) "1989" and "Reputation"

4. Which album won Taylor Swift her first Album of the Year Grammy?
   - A) "Fearless"
   - B) "1989"
   - C) "Red"
   - D) "Folklore"

5. Which Taylor Swift song broke records by staying Number 1 for 6 consecutive weeks?
   - A) "Blank Space"
   - B) "Shake It Off"
   - C) "Out of the Woods"
   - D) "All Too Well (10 Minute Version)"

6. Who is considered the primary producer for Taylor Swift's music?
   - A) Max Martin
   - B) Jack Antonoff
   - C) Dr. Luke
   - D) Rick Rubin

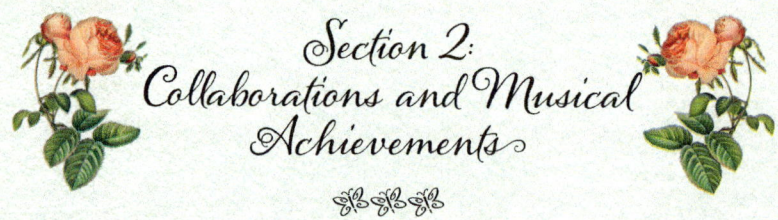

Section 2:
Collaborations and Musical Achievements

7. Who did Taylor Swift collaborate with on the song "Everything Has Changed"?
   - A) Ed Sheeran
   - B) Brendon Urie
   - C) Bon Iver
   - D) Shawn Mendes

8. Which artist did Taylor collaborate with on "ME!"?
   - A) Zac Efron
   - B) Brendon Urie
   - C) Nathan Chapman
   - D) John Mayer

9. What was the first album that featured Taylor Swift writing or co-writing every song?
  - A) "1989"
  - B) "Speak Now"
  - C) "Folklore"
  - D) "Reputation"

10. Which song features the lyric, "I've been the archer, I've been the prey"?
  - A) "The Man"
  - B) "You Need to Calm Down"
  - C) "The Archer"
  - D) "Afterglow"

Section 3:
Fun Facts and Significant Moments

11. How much is Taylor Swift's cat Olivia Benson estimated to be worth, and how does this compare to Travis Kelce's net worth?

  - A) $97 million, more than Travis Kelce's $40 million
  - B) $50 million, less than Travis Kelce's $60 million
  - C) $150 million, twice as much as Travis Kelce's $75 million
  - D) $200 million, equal to Travis Kelce's $200 million

12. At what age did Taylor Swift win her first MTV Video Music Award (VMA)?
  - A) 17
  - B) 19
  - C) 21
  - D) 23

13. Which song is rumored to be about her relationship with Harry Styles?
   - A) "Style"
   - B) "Dear John"
   - C) "We Are Never Ever Getting Back Together"
   - D) "I Knew You Were Trouble"

14. What is Taylor Swift's favorite food?
   - A) Cheesecake
   - B) Burrito
   - C) Chicken tenders
   - D) Pizza

15. How many private jets does Taylor Swift own?
   - A) 1
   - B) 2
   - C) 3
   - D) None

Section 4: Advocacy, Activism, and Influence

16. What significant philanthropic act did Taylor Swift undertake for Nashville flood relief?
   - A) Donated $250,000
   - B) Held a benefit concert
   - C) Donated $500,000
   - D) Organized a charity auction

17. What major music industry confrontation did Taylor have with Kanye West?
    - A) The 2007 Grammy Awards confrontation
    - B) Their collaboration on the song "Famous"
    - C) The 2009 MTV Video Music Awards (VMA) incident
    - D) The 2012 American Music Awards incident

18. In which documentary does Taylor Swift discuss her life, career, and political activism?
    - A) "The Taylor Swift Story"
    - B) "Reputation: The Movie"
    - C) "Taylor Swift: Journey to Fearless"
    - D) "Miss Americana"

19. Taylor has stood against music streaming services' policies in defense of which principle?
    - A) Lower subscription fees
    - B) Higher royalties for artists
    - C) Free access for all listeners
    - D) Exclusive album releases

20. What significant societal issue did Taylor address in her song "You Need to Calm Down"?
    - A) Climate change
    - B) LGBTQ+ rights and acceptance
    - C) Mental health awareness
    - D) Gun control laws

Section 5: Albums and Music Contributions

21. What was Taylor Swift's debut single?
   - A) "Teardrops on My Guitar"
   - B) "Tim McGraw"
   - C) "Our Song"
   - D) "Love Story"

22. Which Taylor Swift song became the first country song to reach number one on the Billboard Pop Songs chart?
   - A) "Our Song"
   - B) "You Belong with Me"
   - C) "Mean"
   - D) "Fearless"

23. Which album marked Taylor's full transition from country to pop music?
   - A) "Speak Now"
   - B) "Red"
   - C) "1989"
   - D) "Reputation"

24. Which song won Taylor Swift her first Grammy for Album of the Year?
   - A) "Fearless"
   - B) "Red"
   - C) "1989"
   - D) "Lover"

25. For which song did Taylor Swift release a 10-minute version in the re-recorded "Red (Taylor's Version)"?
   - A) "State of Grace"
   - B) "Begin Again"
   - C) "We Are Never Ever Getting Back Together"
   - D) "All Too Well"

26. Who did Taylor Swift collaborate with for the song "Exile" on her album "Folklore"?
   - A) Aaron Dessner
   - B) Bon Iver
   - C) The National
   - D) William Bowery

27. What is the theme of Taylor Swift's song "The Man"?
   - A) Environmental awareness
   - B) Gender equality and double standards
   - C) Fame and success
   - D) Love and heartbreak

28. Which Taylor Swift album includes the track "Blank Space"?
   - A) "Speak Now"
   - B) "Red"
   - C) "1989"
   - D) "Lover"

29. Which artist did Taylor Swift collaborate with on the remix of "Bad Blood"?
   - A) Katy Perry
   - B) Kendrick Lamar
   - C) Ed Sheeran
   - D) Zayn Malik

30. What was the lead single from Taylor Swift's album "Reputation"?
- A) "Look What You Made Me Do"
- B) "Delicate"
- C) "End Game"
- D) "Ready for It?"

Section 6: Public Appearances and Performances

31. In which city did Taylor Swift perform during her record-breaking "1989 World Tour"?
- A) Tokyo
- B) Sydney
- C) New York
- D) London

32. How many times has Taylor Swift performed on "Saturday Night Live"?
- A) 1 time
- B) 3 times
- C) 5 times
- D) 7 times

33. During which major event did Taylor Swift fall off a treadmill in a hilariously memorable Apple Music commercial?
- A) The Super Bowl
- B) The Oscars
- C) The Grammys
- D) The VMAs

34. What was unique about the audience's participation during Taylor Swift's "Reputation Stadium Tour"?
    - A) Fans were required to wear specific outfits
    - B) Special light-up wristbands were given to everyone
    - C) Each concert had a different setlist
    - D) There were guest appearances at every show

35. At which award show did Taylor Swift perform "All Too Well (10 Minute Version)" in 2021?
    - A) MTV VMAs
    - B) GRAMMYs
    - C) AMAs
    - D) SNL

Section 7: Business Ventures and Merchandise

36. Which magazine did Taylor Swift partner with to release a special edition including her exclusive content?
    - A) Vogue
    - B) Rolling Stone
    - C) Elle
    - D) TIME

37. What is the name of Taylor Swift's own record label?
    - A) Big Machine Records
    - B) Swift Recordings
    - C) Taylor's Version Records
    - D) Republic Records

38. Which fashion designer has Taylor Swift often collaborated with for tour outfits?
   - A) Michael Kors
   - B) Versace
   - C) Stella McCartney
   - D) Karl Lagerfeld

39. What is the title of Taylor Swift's autobiographical concert film on Netflix?
   - A) "The 1989 World Tour"
   - B) "Reputation Stadium Tour"
   - C) "Miss Americana"
   - D) "Folklore: The Long Pond Studio Sessions"

40. Which brand of fashion did Taylor Swift partner with to create a children's clothing line?
   - A) Brandy Melville
   - B) Urban Outfitters
   - C) KEDS
   - D) Old Navy

41. What was Taylor Swift's first fragrance called?
   - A) "Wonderstruck"
   - B) "Incredible Things"
   - C) "Enchanted"
   - D) "Fame"

42. Which Taylor Swift album was accompanied by a book featuring exclusive photos, journal entries, and paintings?
   - A) "Red"
   - B) "1989"
   - C) "Lover"
   - D) "Folklore"

43. What is the name of Taylor Swift's own cats-inspired merchandise line?
   - A) "Swift Paws"
   - B) "Meredith & Olivia Collection"
   - C) "Kitty World"
   - D) "Caticature"

44. What event did Taylor Swift's "The Swift Life" app focus on?
   - A) Connecting with fans
   - B) Streaming music
   - C) News updates
   - D) Exclusive concerts

45. Taylor Swift has a line of greeting cards produced by which company?
   - A) Hallmark
   - B) American Greetings
   - C) Papyrus
   - D) Carlton Cards

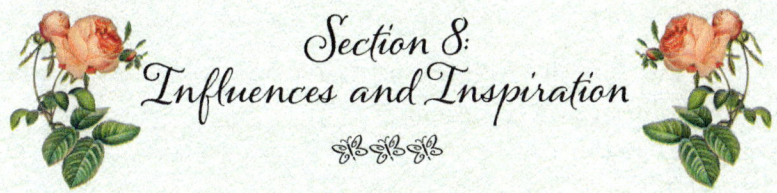

Section 8: Influences and Inspiration

46. Which classic rock band did Taylor Swift name as one of her major influences?
   - A) The Beatles
   - B) Fleetwood Mac
   - C) Eagles
   - D) Rolling Stones

47. What iconic pop star has Taylor Swift often cited as a major inspiration?
   - A) Madonna
   - B) Britney Spears
   - C) Janet Jackson
   - D) Celine Dion

48. Which of her own songs did Taylor Swift describe as her response to disenchantment with the music business?
   - A) "Shake It Off"
   - B) "Mean"
   - C) "The Lucky One"
   - D) "Blank Space"

49. Taylor Swift has revealed that her album "Lover" was influenced by the author Khalil Gibran. Which of his works did she mention?
   - A) "The Prophet"
   - B) "Broken Wings"
   - C) "Sand and Foam"
   - D) "The Madman"

50. Which 90's female singer-songwriter has Taylor Swift credited as a major influence on her music?
   - A) Sheryl Crow
   - B) Jewel
   - C) Alanis Morissette
   - D) Sarah McLachlan

Section 9:
Awards and Recognition

❧❧❧

51. How many Grammy Awards has Taylor Swift won as of 2023?
  - A) 10
  - B) 11
  - C) 12
  - D) 13

52. Which of Taylor Swift's albums was the first to win the Grammy for Album of the Year twice?
  - A) "Fearless" and "1989"
  - B) "Red" and "1989"
  - C) "Speak Now" and "Reputation"
  - D) "Folklore" and "1989"

53. What is the name of the record-breaking achievement Taylor Swift reached in the "Fearless" era?
  - A) Youngest artist to win a Brit Award
  - B) First female artist to win an AMA Artist of the Decade
  - C) Youngest artist to win the Grammy for Album of the Year
  - D) Most Billboard Music Awards in a single year

54. Which Taylor Swift music video won the MTV VMA for Video of the Year in 2019?
  - A) "Look What You Made Me Do"
  - B) "ME!"
  - C) "You Need to Calm Down"
  - D) "Lover"

55. At which awards show did Taylor Swift win "Artist of the Decade" in 2019?
- A) American Music Awards (AMAs)
- B) MTV Video Music Awards (VMAs)
- C) Billboard Music Awards (BBMAs)
- D) Grammy Awards

56. Which of Taylor Swift's songs was nominated for an Academy Award for Best Original Song?
- A) "Safe & Sound"
- B) "Beautiful Ghosts"
- C) "I Don't Wanna Live Forever"
- D) "Sweeter Than Fiction"

57. In what year did Taylor Swift first appear on TIME magazine's list of 100 most influential people?
- A) 2014
- B) 2015
- C) 2016
- D) 2017

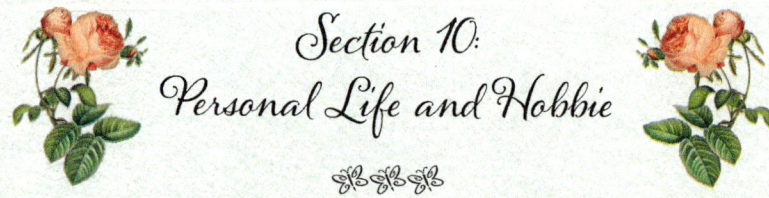

Section 10: Personal Life and Hobbie

58. What is Taylor Swift's favorite number, often seen incorporated into her life and career?
- A) 7
- B) 13
- C) 22
- D) 44

59. What is the name of Taylor Swift's current residence in New York City?
   - A) Tribeca Penthouse
   - B) Greenwich Village Townhouse
   - C) West Village Duplex
   - D) SoHo Apartment

60. Taylor Swift learned to play which musical instrument first?
   - A) Piano
   - B) Guitar
   - C) Banjo
   - D) Violin

Answers:

1. A) "Taylor Swift"
She released her self-titled debut album in 2006. This album marked the beginning of her rise to fame, showcasing her country music roots with hits such as "Tim McGraw" and "Teardrops on My Guitar."

2. C) "Fearless"
"Fearless" was released in 2008 and featured these blockbuster hits. The album solidified Taylor Swift's status as a crossover artist, appealing to both country and pop audiences. "Love Story" and "You Belong with Me" became anthems of their time, showcasing her storytelling ability and relatable lyrics. "Fearless" went on to win numerous awards, including the Grammy Award for Album of the Year.

3. C) "Folklore" and "Evermore"

During the COVID-19 pandemic in 2020, Taylor Swift surprised fans by releasing two albums, "Folklore" in July and "Evermore" in December. These albums marked a significant departure from her previous pop-centric works, dipping into indie-folk and alternative genres. The surprise aspect of the releases was unique since there was minimal promotion prior to their drop, contrasting with the typical months-long buildup for major album releases. "Folklore" and "Evermore" are often described as companion albums because of their cohesive storytelling, introspective lyrics, and atmospheric soundscapes. Both albums received critical acclaim and commercial success, with "Folklore" winning Album of the Year at the 63rd Annual Grammy Awards.

4. A) "Fearless"

"Fearless," Taylor Swift's second studio album, won her the prestigious Album of the Year Grammy at the 52nd Annual Grammy Awards in 2010. Released in 2008, "Fearless" marked a pivotal moment in Swift's career, solidifying her transition from a country music ingénue to a mainstream megastar. The album features hit singles like "Love Story" and "You Belong with Me," which showcased her talent for crafting relatable stories through her music. The Grammy win for Album of the Year made Taylor Swift the youngest artist at the time to receive this accolade, cementing her status as one of the most influential and successful artists in contemporary music. The success of "Fearless" also played a significant role in expanding her fan base and elevating her career to new heights.

5. A) "Blank Space"
This track from her "1989" album stayed at Number 1 for six consecutive weeks on the Billboard Hot 100 chart.

6. B) Jack Antonoff
Jack Antonoff has been a pivotal collaborator in Taylor Swift's music, producing several of her albums including "1989," "Reputation," "Lover," "Folklore," and "Evermore," contributing greatly to her sound evolution.

7. A) Ed Sheeran
Featured on Taylor Swift's 2012 album "Red," "Everything Has Changed" is a heartfelt duet between Taylor Swift and Ed Sheeran. This collaboration came about when Taylor, who was already a fan of Ed's music, approached him to write and perform a song together. Their combined talents as songwriters and singers created a tender ballad that explores the theme of how life changes after meeting someone special. The song became widely appreciated for its lyrical depth and the chemistry between the two artists.

8. B) Brendon Urie
"ME!" is the lead single from Taylor Swift's seventh studio album "Lover," released in 2019. The song features Brendon Urie, the lead vocalist of Panic! At The Disco. Taylor Swift and Brendon Urie co-wrote the track along with Joel Little, and it is noted for its bright, upbeat pop sound and positive message about self-acceptance and

individuality. The colorful and vibrant music video accompanying the track further highlights the playful and joyous nature of the collaboration, making "ME!" a feel-good anthem that emphasizes the unique traits that each person brings to a relationship.

9. B) "Speak Now"
"Speak Now," released in 2010, is unique as Taylor Swift wrote all the songs solely herself, demonstrating her prowess as a songwriter and storyteller.

10. C) "The Archer"
This introspective and emotional song, featured on Taylor Swift's 2019 album "Lover," delves into themes of vulnerability, self-reflection, and personal growth. The lyric captures the duality of Swift's experiences, portraying her as both a fighter and someone who has felt defeated.

11. A) $97 million, more than Travis Kelce's $40 million
Taylor Swift's cat, Olivia Benson, shines with a sparkling $97 million net worth, dwarfing NFL star Travis Kelce's $40 million. Olivia's fortune comes from star-studded ad appearances, proving that a cat's purr-sonality can indeed pay off big time!

12. B) 19
Taylor won her first VMA at age 19 in 2009 for her music video "You Belong with Me," marking a significant milestone early in her career.

13. A) "Style"
"Style" is widely believed to be about her relationship with Harry Styles, as the title cleverly references his last name and the lyrics allude to their iconic on-and-off romance, capturing the essence of their highly publicized relationship.

14. A) Cheesecake
Taylor has mentioned in various interviews and social media posts that she loves cheesecake, often indulging in it as a special treat.

15. B) 2
She owns two private jets, facilitating her global travel needs.

16. C) Donated $500,000
Taylor Swift made a substantial donation of $500,000 to support Nashville flood relief efforts, showcasing her dedication to helping her hometown during times of crisis.

17. C) The 2009 MTV Video Music Awards (VMA) incident

This infamous moment occurred when Kanye West, in a dramatic and highly publicized interruption, stormed the stage during Taylor Swift's acceptance speech for Best Female Video. Kanye grabbed the mic and declared that Beyoncé had one of the best videos of all time, sparking a decade-long saga of memes, celebrity gossip, and public apologies. Who can forget that "Imma let you finish..." line?

18. D) "Miss Americana"

"Miss Americana" takes you on a rollercoaster ride through Taylor Swift's dynamic world, offering a front-row seat to her most candid moments. From detailing her struggles with public persona to her bold political stances, it's like peeking behind the celebrity curtain. Plus, watch her incredible transformation from a country pop princess to a fierce advocate, all wrapped in juicy behind-the-scenes drama and heartfelt revelations. A must-watch for fans and gossip lovers alike!

19. B) Higher royalties for artists

Taylor removed her music from Spotify challenging their compensation model and penned an open letter to Apple Music demanding fair pay during free trials.

20. B) LGBTQ+ rights and acceptance

Taylor Swift's "You Need to Calm Down" is more than just a catchy tune—it's a powerful anthem for LGBTQ+ rights and acceptance. In the song, Taylor takes a stand against hate and ignorance, advocating for love and equality in her signature pop style. The vibrant and colorful music video features appearances by numerous LGBTQ+ celebrities and allies, boldly promoting visibility and inclusivity within the community. With lines addressing social media trolls and promoting unity, not to mention a call to action for the Equality Act, Taylor not only showcases her evolution as an artist but also her growing role as a social activist. This track sparked widespread conversations and showed the world that Queen Tay stands firmly for equality and justice.

21. B) "Tim McGraw"

Released in 2006, "Tim McGraw" was Taylor Swift's debut single.

22. B) "You Belong with Me"

Taylor Swift's "You Belong with Me," from her 2009 album "Fearless," marked a pivotal crossover from country to pop. The song's catchy melody and relatable lyrics about high school love struck a chord with a broad audience, propelling it to the top of the Billboard Pop Songs chart. This success highlighted Taylor's versatility and paved the way for her future as a crossover superstar, blending country storytelling with pop appeal.

23. C) "1989"
"1989" is widely recognized as Taylor Swift's first all-pop album.

24. A) "Fearless"
"Fearless" won Album of the Year at the 2010 Grammy Awards.

25. D) "All Too Well"
Taylor Swift dropped the bombshell 10-minute version of "All Too Well" in "Red (Taylor's Version)," causing an absolute frenzy among fans. Known for its heart-wrenching lyrics and rumored ties to a high-profile relationship, this epic version had everyone grabbing tissues and decoding every line. Rumors and emotions ran wild, making it an instant sensation and giving us all the feels.

26. B) Bon Iver
Bon Iver (Justin Vernon) features on the duet "Exile."

27. B) Gender equality and double standards
In "The Man," Taylor Swift fiercely takes on gender inequality and the double standards women face. She provocatively imagines how her life would differ if she were a man, pointing out the hypocritical way society judges female success. This song is Taylor at her boldest—serving up sass, truth, and girl power all wrapped in a catchy melody.

28. C) "1989"
"Blank Space" was a hit single from "1989."

29. B) Kendrick Lamar
Kendrick Lamar's verses featured on the remix of "Bad Blood."

30. A) "Look What You Made Me Do"
"Look What You Made Me Do" heralded a significant shift in Taylor Swift's musical and thematic style. The lead single introduced the darker, edgier tone of her album "Reputation," with its biting lyrics and vengeful attitude signaling a new era for Taylor. The song's release was accompanied by a high-profile music video that further emphasized the change in her public persona.

31. A) Tokyo
The "1989 World Tour" began in Tokyo, Japan, in May 2015.

32. B) 3 times
Taylor Swift has graced the stage of "Saturday Night Live" three times, reflecting her significant impact on the music industry and popular culture. Her performances on the show have showcased her versatility and ability to engage a live audience, further cementing her status as a leading artist.

33. A) The Super Bowl
Taylor Swift's comedic tumble off a treadmill in the Apple Music commercial premiered during the Super Bowl, one of the most-watched events of the year. The ad was a big hit, showcasing her playful side and generating a lot of buzz and laughs.

34. B) Special light-up wristbands were given to everyone
Every concertgoer received special light-up wristbands that synced with the music, creating a stunning and interactive light show throughout the stadium. It added a magical and immersive element to the experience, making each fan feel like a part of the spectacle.

35. D) SNL
Taylor Swift's extended performance of "All Too Well (10 Minute Version)" captivated audiences and was featured live on "Saturday Night Live," showcasing her storytelling and emotional depth in a live setting.

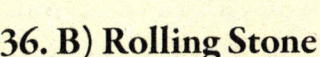

36. B) Rolling Stone
Taylor Swift has launched special editions of Rolling Stone, providing fans with a deep dive into her life, music, and career through exclusive content and interviews presented in the magazine.

37. D) Republic Records
Taylor Swift signed with Republic Records when she transitioned from Big Machine Records.

38. C) Stella McCartney
Taylor Swift and Stella McCartney have formed a close collaborative relationship, particularly noted during Taylor's "Lover" era. The two teamed up to create a collection that merges McCartney's sophisticated, yet playful style with Swift's distinct fashion persona. This collaboration was highlighted by exclusive merchandise and clothing lines inspired by Swift's "Lover" album, showcasing beautifully designed pieces that provided a visual representation of Taylor's artistic vision. Their partnership exemplifies a fusion of high fashion and music, leading to a celebrated and well-received line that fans and fashion enthusiasts alike have admired.

39. C) "Miss Americana"
"Miss Americana" is a deeply personal and revealing documentary film that offers an introspective look into Taylor Swift's life and career. Directed by Lana Wilson, the film premiered on Netflix in January 2020. Unlike a traditional concert film, "Miss Americana" explores beyond the stage and provides a candid look at Swift's personal experiences, her artistic evolution, and the challenges she has faced in the public eye. The documentary covers significant moments in Swift's career, including her decision to become more politically outspoken, her battles with the media, and her efforts to redefine her place in the music industry. By showcasing her vulnerabilities and strengths, "Miss Americana" presents a multifaceted portrait of Taylor Swift, both as an artist and as a person.

40. C) KEDS

Taylor Swift partnered with KEDS, the iconic American shoe brand, to create various collections primarily aimed at young women rather than children specifically. This partnership, which began in 2012, underwent multiple collaborations showcasing Swift's sense of style, featuring her signature touches. The collections included a variety of sneaker designs that often incorporated her favorite colors, patterns, and inspiration from her albums. Each design aimed to merge comfort with style, reflecting Swift's own personal fashion sense while making practical and appealing footwear for a wider demographic, including younger audiences. In addition to her collections with KEDS, Taylor Swift has been known to partner with other brands and designers to extend her influence in the fashion world, further cementing her status as a style icon.

41. A) "Wonderstruck"

Taylor Swift launched her first fragrance, "Wonderstruck," in 2011. The name "Wonderstruck" is derived from the lyrics of her song "Enchanted" from her third studio album, *Speak Now*. The fragrance represents the feeling of being captivated and the sensation Taylor describes in the song.

42. C) "Lover"

The "Lover" Deluxe Album, released in 2019, included a book with exclusive content such as photos, personal journal entries, and Taylor's own paintings. This special edition provided fans with a more intimate look into her creative process and personal life, offering a unique and deeply personal accompaniment to the music of the "Lover" album.

43. B) "Meredith & Olivia Collection"
Taylor Swift's cats-inspired merchandise line is named the "Meredith & Olivia Collection," after her two famous cats, Meredith Grey and Olivia Benson. This collection features a variety of items that celebrate her love for her pets.

44. A) Connecting with fans
"The Swift Life" app was like a magical digital playground for Swifties! Launched in late 2017, this app was specifically designed to bring Taylor Swift closer to her beloved fans. Imagine a virtual world sprinkled with all things Taylor—exclusive photos, videos, and voice notes directly from the pop sensation herself. Fans could interact with each other, share their own creations, like drawings or covers of Taylor's songs, and earn *Taymojis* (Taylor-themed emojis) to express their excitement.

45. B) American Greetings
Taylor Swift's collaboration with American Greetings brought her personal touch to the world of greeting cards. These cards are sprinkled with her unique style and charm, perfect for any Swiftie occasion. Whether it's a heartfelt birthday wish or a quirky thank you note, Taylor's creative flair lets you share sentiments with a dash of her magic!

46. B) Fleetwood Mac
Taylor Swift admires Fleetwood Mac, especially their storytelling and musical style, which significantly influenced her own songwriting and creative process.

47. A) Madonna
Taylor Swift has often cited Madonna as a major inspiration for her career, especially admiring Madonna's ability to continually reinvent herself and remain relevant in the ever-changing music industry. Madonna has been a trailblazer in pushing the boundaries of music, fashion, and culture for several decades, which resonates deeply with Taylor's own ambitions. In various interviews, Taylor has credited Madonna's transformative style and fearless approach to artistry as motivating factors in her own bold career choices.

48. C) "The Lucky One"
"The Lucky One," a track from Taylor Swift's critically acclaimed album "Red," delves into the darker aspects of fame that are often glossed over. While on the surface, being famous may appear glamorous, Swift reveals the isolation, relentless scrutiny, and loss of privacy that accompany stardom. The song narrates the story of someone who seemingly has it all but ends up disenchanted with the music industry. This reflective piece showcases Swift's insightful commentary on the fleeting nature of fame and the personal sacrifices involved. Her poignant lyrics are aimed at highlighting the price of success and serve as a cautionary tale that resonates not only with aspiring artists but also with her fans, offering a more realistic perspective on what it means to be "The Lucky One." Through this song, Swift expresses empathy for those who step away from the limelight to preserve their mental health and personal well-being.

49. A) "The Prophet"
Taylor Swift cited "The Prophet," Khalil Gibran's renowned philosophical work, as an inspiration for her album "Lover." The book,

known for its poetic musings on love, life, and human experiences, resonates deeply with the themes explored throughout Swift's record. "Lover" encapsulates a panorama of emotions and relationships, much like Gibran's reflective and spiritually rich prose. By incorporating Gibran's introspective and timeless wisdom, Swift infuses her lyrics with a sense of depth and contemplation, bridging the poetic eloquence of Gibran with the modern narrative of her own experiences and observations on love and life.

50. C) Alanis Morissette

Alanis Morissette's emotional vulnerability and raw honesty in her songwriting have significantly inspired Taylor Swift. Morissette's powerful and conversational style, particularly evident in her album "Jagged Little Pill," encouraged Swift to embrace personal narratives and emotional candor in her own music, driving both connection with her audience and exploration of complex emotional landscapes.

51. B) 11

Taylor Swift has accumulated a total of 11 Grammy Awards as of 2023, reflecting her extraordinary talent and impact on the music industry. Her accolades include prestigious categories such as Album of the Year, which she has won multiple times. These awards highlight her versatility and consistent excellence as an artist across different genres and projects.

52. A) "Fearless" and "1989"

Taylor Swift achieved a significant milestone in her career with her albums "Fearless" and "1989," both of which won the Grammy Award for Album of the Year. "Fearless" captured the award in 2010, establishing her as a major force in the music industry, and "1989" followed with a win in 2016, further cementing her reputation for creating critically acclaimed and commercially successful albums.

53. C) Youngest artist to win the Grammy for Album of the Year

During the "Fearless" era, Taylor Swift achieved the remarkable record of being the youngest artist to win the Grammy Award for Album of the Year. This milestone occurred at the 52nd Annual Grammy Awards held in 2010 when she was just 20 years old, making her the youngest artist to ever receive this prestigious honor at that time. This accolade marked a significant point in her career, highlighting her as a rising star in the music industry.

54. C) "You Need to Calm Down"

The video was acclaimed for its strong social message supporting the LGBTQ+ community and won the award in 2019.

55. A) American Music Awards (AMAs)

Taylor Swift won "Artist of the Decade" at the 2019 American Music Awards (AMAs). This fan-voted award recognized her immense influence and success throughout the 2010s, with chart-topping albums and countless hits. During the event, she performed a medley of her greatest songs, solidifying her status as a pop icon. The AMAs celebrate artists primarily based on fan engagement, making this accolade a true testament to her dedicated fanbase.

56. B) "Beautiful Ghosts"
"Beautiful Ghosts," co-written by Taylor Swift and Andrew Lloyd Webber, was nominated for an Academy Award for Best Original Song. It was specifically composed for the 2019 film adaptation of the musical "Cats." Known for her versatile songwriting skills, Taylor's contribution to this project demonstrated her ability to seamlessly transition from pop and country genres to theatrical music. Despite the film's mixed reviews, "Beautiful Ghosts" earned recognition for its lyrical and melodic quality, highlighting Taylor Swift's enduring talent and expanding her achievements into the realm of film music.

57. B) 2015
Taylor Swift first appeared on TIME magazine's list of the 100 most influential people in 2015, a significant milestone in her career.

58. B) 13
Certainly! Taylor Swift considers 13 her lucky number and frequently incorporates it into her life and career. For instance, she was born on December 13th, and many noteworthy events in her career occurred on the 13th or involve the number 13. She even writes the number on her hand before performing. Swift views the number as a symbol of good

fortune and a token of personal significance, reflecting her belief that the number has brought her luck and success. This deep connection to 13 is a charming idiosyncrasy that fans have come to recognize and celebrate.

59. A) Tribeca Penthouse

Certainly! Taylor Swift's current residence in New York City is a penthouse located in the Tribeca neighborhood. She purchased this luxurious penthouse in 2014 and has since transformed it into a remarkable living space. Tribeca is known for its trendy vibe and has become a popular spot for many celebrities. Swift's residence in Tribeca is more than just a home; it's also a part of her identity as an artist who values privacy alongside her vibrant public life. Her penthouse is often noted for its stylish and chic decor, embodying Swift's personal taste and penchant for turning living spaces into warm, inviting places.

60. B) Guitar

Taylor Swift learned to play the guitar early in her career, which significantly influenced her songwriting.

Scoring and Results

After tallying up your points, see which category best describes your Taylor Swift knowledge:

0-15 Points: Newbie Swiftie
Welcome to the world of Taylor Swift! You're just starting on your journey, but there's plenty to discover. Dive into her albums, explore her music videos, and learn about her incredible career. With some time and a bit of Swiftie dedication, you'll be climbing the ranks in no time!

16-30 Points: Aspiring Swiftie
You're getting there! While you've grasped some basic details about Taylor Swift, there's still a lot more to unravel. Keep exploring her discography, lyrics, and the stories behind her songs. Your passion for her music is bound to grow, and soon you'll know even more of the intricate details.

31-45 Points: Aficionado Swiftie
You know your Taylor trivia well! Your impressive knowledge shows a deep appreciation for her artistry. Continue to indulge in Taylor Swift's discography, re-watch her iconic performances, and be updated with her latest endeavors. The fine points are what separate the aficionados from the experts!

46-60 Points: Expert Swiftie
You are a top-tier Swiftie, possessing extensive knowledge about Taylor Swift's career, music, and impact. Whether it's recalling her significant milestones or knowing intricate details about her personal and professional life, your expertise is outstanding. Celebrate your vast Taylor Swift knowledge and stay enthusiastic for what comes next in her phenomenal journey!

LILY F. SMITH

Reflections on Taylor Swift's Influence

Empowering Fans Everywhere

Taylor Swift isn't just a singer; she's a source of inspiration! Through her music and her actions, she empowers people to be proud of who they are and reach for their dreams. Take her song "Mean," for example. It talks about dealing with bullies and standing up for yourself. Lots of fans feel a strong connection to lyrics like these, knowing that Taylor understands their struggles.

But Taylor doesn't stop at music. She's also a fierce advocate for important causes. She supports LGBTQ+ rights and fights for gender equality, urging fans to speak up and take action. By doing so, she spreads messages of love and acceptance, making sure everyone feels included and understood.

In her music videos and concerts, she celebrates diversity by featuring people from all walks of life. Whether it's different cultures or unique experiences, Taylor's inclusiveness shows she cares about everyone feeling seen and valued.

Shake It Up: Changing the Music Industry

Taylor Swift isn't afraid to shake things up! She's always challenging the music industry to be better. When she switched record labels to get more control over her music, it was a big deal. And when she decided to re-record her old albums, she set an example for artists everywhere, showing that they deserve to own their work.

Her stand against unfair streaming services was revolutionary too. In 2015, she pulled her music from Spotify because artists weren't getting paid fairly. This bold move sparked a big conversation about how musicians get paid in the digital age, leading to changes that benefit all artists.

Taylor is also a savvy businesswoman. Her Eras Tour was not just a musical hit but a marketing marvel. Using social media to connect with fans and promote her work, she's set new industry standards that others now follow.

A Legacy in the Making

Taylor Swift has already made her mark on music history with her countless hits and legendary albums. She seamlessly switches from country to pop to indie folk, proving her versatility and dedication to her craft.

Her fight for artists' rights will likely be a huge part of her lasting legacy. By pushing for fairer deals and transparent contracts, she's paving the way for future musicians to have a better, fairer industry.

And it's not just about the music. Taylor's impact could grow even bigger through her activism and philanthropy. From supporting political causes to donating to charities, she's poised to use her voice for good in many ways.

A Global Icon

Taylor's magic isn't limited to one country—she's beloved all around the world! Her songs touch hearts globally because they explore universal feelings like love, heartbreak, and empowerment.

Collaborating with international artists like Ed Sheeran and Zayn Malik has helped Taylor reach even more fans. These musical partnerships showcase her adaptability and eagerness to explore new creative paths.

Her world tours, like the blockbuster Eras Tour, prove her international appeal. Selling out stadiums across the globe, she connects with a wide array of fans, making her a true global phenomenon.

Taylor Swift's influence is vast and far-reaching. Through her music, activism, and heartfelt connections with fans, she continues to inspire people everywhere to dream big, stand up for what they believe in, and embrace their authentic selves.

Learning about Taylor Swift's awesome career and personal journey will totally boost your fan game and give you a whole new level of appreciation for this superstar!

And that's a wrap for this chapter, Swifties! We took a super fun, quiz-filled journey into Taylor Swift's amazing life and career. We chatted about her musical evolution, from her country roots to her dazzling pop hits, and her dreamy indie folk sounds in *"Folklore"* and *"Evermore."* Each change in her music shows how much she's grown and experimented as an artist. From iconic hits like *"Love Story"* and *"Shake It Off"* to hidden gems, we tested our knowledge and celebrated her magical tunes.

We also remembered her cool collabs with stars like Ed Sheeran and Brendon Urie. These team-ups

not only switch up her style but show her huge influence in the music world. Discovering who she's worked with added more layers of awesome to our Taylor appreciation.

You know what's even cooler about Tay? Her lyrics! We connected lines from her songs to different vibes in her career, from young love to more thoughtful themes in her recent work. It was like seeing her life story through songs about love, heartbreak, and superhero-level empowerment.

We dug deeper into the stories behind the lyrics, finding out how her real-life ups and downs inspire her music. Her friendships, love stories, and even her epic comebacks are all part of her narrative, showing her strength and her power to inspire.

But wait, there's more! Taylor's not just a music queen; she's a champion for causes that matter. She's rallied her fans to speak up on important issues, proving she's all about making a difference. Her charity work shows her heart is as big as her talent.

Sprinkled throughout the chapter were fun facts and trivia. Whether it's her speedy songwriting or spotting her in movie cameos, these tidbits make her even more fascinating. And let's not forget the Easter eggs she loves to hide, creating a special game between her and her most loyal fans.

By reflecting on all these incredible moments, not only do we get smarter about our favorite star, but we also feel closer to her story. Taylor's journey is packed with creativity, challenges, and big wins, and we can't wait to see where she goes next.

As we end this exciting chapter, think about all the cool stuff we've uncovered. Taylor's saga isn't just about her songs; it's about her adventures, her grit, and the special ties she forms with her fans. What's coming up for Taylor? Only time will tell, but one thing's for sure: she'll keep enchanting us with her tales. The future's a blank page, ready for more of Taylor's awesome stories!

So keep listening to her music, find the hidden messages, and stay tuned for more exciting things from Taylor Swift! What new chapters will she write, and how will they inspire us? The adventure is just beginning!

Chapter 4

CREATIVE COLORING

Unleash your artistic side with Taylor Swift-inspired coloring pages! We recommend using only colored pencils to bring Taylor's world to life with your unique touch. Each page is a celebration of color and creativity, just like Taylor herself!

Lily F. Smith
101 Captivating Facts About Taylor Swift

Lily F. Smith
101 Captivating Facts About Taylor Swift

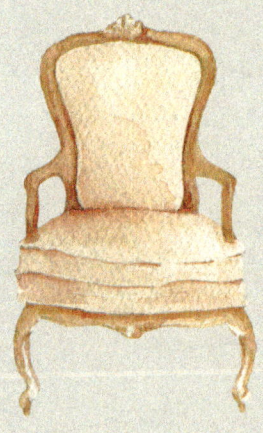

Lily F. Smith
101 Captivating Facts About Taylor Swift

Lily F. Smith
101 Captivating Facts About Taylor Swift

Lily F. Smith
101 Captivating Facts About Taylor Swift

Lily F. Smith
101 Captivating Facts About Taylor Swift

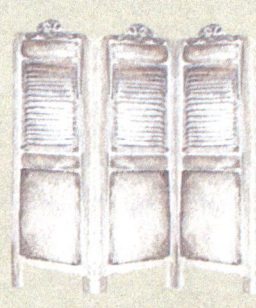

Lily F. Smith
101 Captivating Facts About Taylor Swift

Lily F. Smith
101 Captivating Facts About Taylor Swift

Lily F. Smith
101 Captivating Facts About Taylor Swift

Printed in Great Britain
by Amazon